interpretations

Volume 1

by joji locatelli and veera välimäki

photographs by rafael delceggio

POM POM PRESS

LONDON

Published in 2016 by the Pom Pom Press

Text © 2016 Joji Locatelli & Veera Välimäki

Photographs © 2016 Rafael Delceggio

ISBN: 978-0-9934866-1-6

A catalogue record for this book is available
from the British Library.

Editors: Meghan Fernandes & Lydia Gluck

Associate Editor: Amy Collins

Printed in the UK by Park Communications

POM POM PRESS

B203 Lighthouse Space
89A Shacklewell Lane
London E8 2EB
United Kingdom
pompommag.com

contents

foreword

This is the story of two friends from opposite sides of the world, who met one day with a shared dream. This dream, this idea, this fabulous project, slowly started to take shape.

When we started to get to know each other, we realized we had so many things in common. We shared ideas, concepts and styles, and our dream was to create a small collection of our own, where we could show this all.

For this collection, we chose six themes, six words with a strong meaning for us, either visual or spiritual. There are two designs for each of the six themes, and they show our personal take on each of these words.

Building this up was wonderful, watching ideas and interpretations slowly turn into beautiful knitted garments. It was incredible to see everything become this wonderful and balanced little collection.

It took us some time to finish. A time when we learned from each other, from our countries, our cultures, our differences and similarities, and from the design process itself. A time when our friendship grew big and strong, opening the door to more dreams and plans.

When the work was done, it all came together in our magical photo-shoot, which took place in Argentina. It was the way this journey was bound to be finished: with our first real meeting.

This project has been full of joy, happiness and laughter, with a few occasional start-overs. We hope to inspire you with our first collaborative design work, and we hope some of all the love we have put in it shows through these brief pages.

happy knitting,
joji and veera

subtle

Everyone needs a little subtleness sometimes. It is about striking a balance in everything you do between too much and not enough. It is just beneath the surface and if you don't try you might not see it. Seeing it isn't always the answer though, since each piece plays a unique part and in the end, without it, something will apparently be missing. We hope to make pieces that can be striking and then some that are subtle since each day brings new feelings and a new you. Subtle is just the beginning of much more that has yet to come.

subtle

feather and cloud cardigan

sweet cables pullover

sweet cables

by joji locatelli

This sweet pullover combines superior comfort with feminine
shaping. The relaxed cables in the collar and the rounded back
hem create a mellow vibe on this basic layering garment. Worked
from the top down in one piece in a flowy and drapey yarn,
this quick sweater will sure be one of your favorites.

sweet cables

Sizes

To fit chest: 30/32 (34/36, 38/40, 42/44, 46/48, 50/52, 54/56)"; 75/80 (85/90, 95/100, 105/110, 115/120, 125/130, 135/140) cm. *Note: See more detailed finished measurements below in schematics picture or written on page 17.*

Materials

Yarn: 6 (6, 7, 8, 8, 9, 10) skeins of Silky Merino by Malabrigo (51% silk / 49% merino; 150 yd [137 m] - 50g). Shown in colorway Cape Cod Gray, in size 34/36.
Needles: US 6 (4 mm) and US 4 (3.5 mm) circular needles.
Other: Cable needle, row counter (optional), crochet hook, and waste yarn for provisional cast on.

Gauge

19 st and 28 rows = 4" [10 cm] on US 6 [4 mm] needles, in Stockinette stitch, after blocking.

Finished Measurements

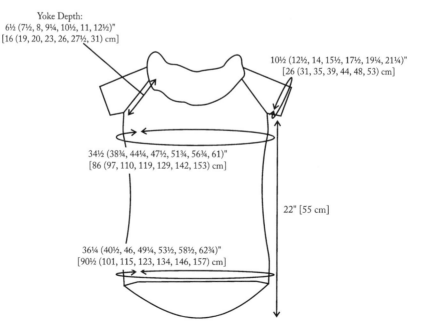

Yoke Depth:
6½ (7½, 8, 9¼, 10½, 11, 12½)"
[16 (19, 20, 23, 26, 27½, 31) cm]

10½ (12½, 14, 15½, 17½, 19¼, 21¼)"
[26 (31, 35, 39, 44, 48, 53) cm]

34½ (38¾, 44¼, 47½, 51¾, 56¾, 61)"
[86 (97, 110, 119, 129, 142, 153) cm]

22" [55 cm]

36¼ (40½, 46, 49¼, 53½, 58½, 62¾)"
[90½ (101, 115, 123, 134, 146, 157) cm]

sweet cables

Neckband

Provisionally CO 44.

> *Row 1 (RS):* P2, k to end.
>
> *Row 2 (WS):* K2, p to 2 st from end, k2.

Work *rows 1-2* — 5 more times.

> *Row 13:* P2, C20F (slip 10 onto the CN, hold in front, k10, k10 from CN), k to end.
>
> *Row 14:* K2, p to 2 st from end, k2.

Work row *rows 1-2* — 8 times.

> *Row 31:* P2, k20, C20B (slip 10 onto the CN, hold in back, k10, k10 from CN), k2.
>
> *Row 32:* K2, p to 2 st from end, k2.

Work *rows 1-2* twice.

Work this 36-row sequence a total of 5 (5, 6, 6, 6, 7, 7) times. *You should have worked 180 (180, 216, 216, 216, 252, 252) rows.*

Unravel your provisional stitches, and graft both ends of your piece together, making sure the piece is not twisted.

Body of the sweater

Starting at the seam of your neckband, pick up and knit 90 (90, 108, 108, 108, 126, 126) stitches along the right edge of your neckband (pick up 1 st for every 2 rows) and place markers the following way:

> Pick up 15 (15, 18, 18, 18, 21, 21), pm, pick up 10 (10, 13, 13, 13, 16, 16), pm, pick up 40 (40, 46, 46, 46, 52, 52), pm, pick up 10 (10, 13, 13, 13, 16, 16), pm, pick up 15 (15, 18, 18, 18, 21, 21).

When you finish picking up stitches, you should be at your seam again, and ready for knitting in the round. Do NOT place a marker here, since this will not be the beginning of your rounds.

Shape neckline and establish raglan increases (back and forth):

> *Row 1 (RS):* K to 1st marker, sm, wrap next stitch and turn (W&T – see Glossary).
>
> *Row 2 (WS):* Sm, purl to next marker, sm, W&T.
>
> *Row 3:* Sm, k1, m1L, k to 1 st before marker, m1R, k1, sm, k next st together with wrap, k1, W&T.
>
> *Row 4:* P to marker, sm, p to next marker, sm, p next st together with wrap, p1, W&T.
>
> *Row 5:* *K to 1 st before marker, m1R, k1, sm, k1, m1L* twice, k to wrapped st and k it tog with wrap, k1, W&T.

You should now have 34 (34, 40, 40, 40, 46, 46) st for the back section and 11 (11, 14, 14, 14, 17, 17) st for each sleeve.

> *Row 6:* P to wrapped st and purl it tog with

wrap, p1, W&T.

Row 7: *K to 1 st before marker, m1R, k1, sm, k1, m1L* twice, k to wrapped st and k it tog with wrap, k2, W&T.

Row 8: P to wrapped st and purl it tog with wrap, p2, W&T.

Row 9: *K to 1 st before marker, m1R, k1, sm, k1, m1L* twice, k to wrapped st and k it tog with wrap, k to marker, sm, W&T.

You should now have 38 (38, 44, 44, 44, 50, 50) for the back section and 13 (13, 16, 16, 16, 19, 19) for each sleeve.

Row 10: Sm, p to wrapped st and purl it tog with wrap, p to next marker, sm, W&T.

Row 11: Sm, k1, m1L, *k to 1 st before next m, m1R, k1, sm, k1, m1L* twice, k to 1 st before next m, m1R, k1, sm, pick up wrap and k it with its corresponding st, k1, W&T.

Row 12: P to wrapped st and purl it tog with wrap, p1, W&T.

Row 13: *K to 1 st before next marker, m1R, k1, sm, k1, m1L* 4 times, k to wrapped st and work it tog with wrap, k1, W&T.

You should now have 42 (42, 48, 48, 48, 54, 54) for front and back, and 17 (17, 20, 20, 20, 23, 23) for each sleeve.

Row 14: P to wrapped st, p it together with wrap, p1, W&T.

Repeat *rows 13 and 14* — 4 more times.

You should have a total of 150 (150, 168, 168, 168, 186, 186) st: 50 (50, 56, 56, 56, 62, 62) st for the front and the back and 25 (25, 28, 28, 28, 31, 31) st for each sleeve.

On the next row you will start knitting in the round — Subtle garter round: *K to 1 st before next marker, m1R, k1, sm, k1, m1L* 4 times, k 17 (17, 19, 19, 19, 21, 21) (pick up wrap and knit it together with its corresponding st as you find it). Kfbf 3 (3, 4, 4, 4, 5, 5) times, k3, kfbf 2 (2, 4, 4, 4, 4, 4) times, k3, kfbf 3 (3, 4, 4, 4, 5, 5) times. K to next marker (pick up wrap and knit it together with its corresponding st as you find it). This will be the new beginning of the round.

You should have a total of 174 (174, 200, 200, 200, 222, 222) st: 52 (52, 58, 58, 58, 64, 64) st for the back, 27 (27, 30, 30, 30, 33, 33) for each sleeve and 68 (68, 82, 82, 82, 92, 92) st for the front.

Next Raglan round 1: K to 1 st before the end of round, m1R, k1.

Next Raglan round 2: *K1, m1L, k to 1 st before next marker, m1R, k1, sm* 3 times, k1, m1L, k to end of round.

Repeat *raglan rounds 1 and 2* — 9 (13, 15, 18, 22, 24, 29) more times.

You should have 72 (80, 90, 96, 104, 114, 124) for the back, 47 (55, 62, 68, 76, 83, 93) st for each sleeve and 88 (96, 114, 120, 128, 142, 152) for the front.

Divide for body and sleeves

Next round (remove sleeve markers as you find them): Slip the next 47 (55, 62, 68, 76, 83, 93) st onto a piece of waste yarn. Using backwards loop CO 1 (2, 2, 3, 4, 4, 4), pm (beginning of round), CO 1 (2, 2, 3, 4, 4, 4) more. Knit across the back stitches. Slip the next 47 (55, 62, 68, 76, 83, 93) st onto a piece of waste yarn. CO 1 (2, 2, 3, 4, 4, 4), pm (2nd side marker), CO 1 (2, 2, 3, 4, 4, 4) more. Knit to end.

You should have 164 (184, 212, 228, 248, 272, 292) st for the body — 74 (84, 94, 102, 112, 122, 132) for the back and 90 (100, 118, 126, 136, 150, 160) for the front.

Knit 30 rounds.

Waist shaping

Next round: Ssk, knit to 2 st before next marker, k2tog, sm, ssk, k to 2 st before m, k2tog.

Continue working in Stockinette and repeat the decrease row every 12th round 1 more time.

Knit 12 rounds.

Next round: (Knit to 1 st before next marker, m1R, k1, sm, k1, m1L) twice, knit to the end of round.

Continue working in Stockinette and repeat the increase row every 10th row 3 more times.

You should have a total of 172 (192, 220, 236, 256, 280, 300) st.

Bottom shaping

When work measures 16" [40 cm] from the armhole, start bottom shaping, working back and forth.

Row 1: K to next marker (2nd side marker), sm, k6, m1L, W&T.

Row 2: P to beginning of the round marker, p6, m1Lp, W&T.

Row 3 (Slip markers as you find them): K to 5 st before last wrapped st (on the left needle you should have 5 st and then the wrapped st), m1L, W&T.

Row 4 (Slip markers as you find them): P to 5 st before last wrapped st (on the left needle you should have 5 st and then the wrapped st), m1Lp, W&T.

Repeat *rows 3 and 4* once.

Row 7: K to 2 st before last wrapped st, m1L, W&T.

Row 8: P to 2 st before last wrapped st, m1Lp, W&T.

Repeat *rows 7 and 8* — 5 times more.

Row 19: K to 3 st before last wrapped st, m1L, W&T.

Row 20: P to 3 st before last wrapped st, m1Lp, W&T.

Repeat *rows 19 and 20* once.

Row 23: K to 4 st before last wrapped st, m1L, W&T.

Row 24: P to 4 st before last wrapped st, m1Lp, W&T.

Row 25: K to 6 st before last wrapped st, m1L, W&T.

Row 26: P to 6 st before last wrapped st, m1Lp, W&T.

Row 27 (Slipping markers): K to last wrapped st (from row 1) picking up wraps and knitting them tog with their corresponding st (including last wrapped st), W&T.

Row 28 (Slipping markers): P to last wrapped st (from row 2) picking up wraps and purling them tog with their corresponding st (including last wrapped st), W&T.

Row 29: K to "beginning of round marker", sm, switch to US 4 [3.5 mm] needles. *k1, p1*, repeat to the end of round.

Work 4 more rounds in k1, p1 ribbing. On the next round bind off all st.

Sleeves

Place the held stitches from one of the sleeves onto a needle. Join yarn to work a RS round.

Knit all stitches, pick up and knit 1 (2, 2, 3, 4, 4, 4) stitches from the stitches you cast on at underarm, pm, pick up and knit 1 (2, 2, 3, 4, 4, 4) more stitches.

You should have 49 (59, 66, 74, 84, 91, 101) stitches.

Knit 6 rounds.

Next round: knit to 2 st before marker, ssk, sm, k2tog (2 stitches decreased).

Knit 6 rounds.

Sizes 30/32, 34/36, 50/52 and 54/56 only:

Next round: K2tog, p1 *k1, p1*, repeat to the end of round.

Sizes 38/40, 42/44, 46/48 only:

Next round: *K1, p1*, repeat to the end of round.

All sizes:

Work 4 more rounds of (k1, p1) ribbing. On the next round bind off all st in pattern.

Finishing

Weave in ends and block lightly.

Finished Measurements

Bust circumference (incl. subtle gathers): 34½ (38¾, 44¼, 47½, 51¾, 56¾, 61)" [86 (97, 110, 119, 129, 142, 153) cm].

Bottom hem circumference: 36¼ (40½, 46, 49¼, 53½, 58½, 62¾)" [90½ (101, 115, 123, 134, 146, 157) cm].

Yoke depth (excluding cowl neck): 6½ (7½, 8, 9¼, 10½, 11, 12½)" [16 (19, 20, 23, 26, 27½, 31) cm].

Upper sleeve circumference: 10½ (12½, 14, 15½, 17½, 19¼, 21¼)" [26 (31, 35, 39, 44, 48, 53) cm].

Sleeve length from underarm to cuff: 2¼" [6 cm].

Length from underarm to bottom measured at the back: 22" [55 cm].

feather and cloud

by veera välimäki

Squishy garter stitch, feather and fan pattern and soft
reversed Stockinette stitch with small details meet in
this lovely open cardigan. Subtle shaping at the waist and
3/4- sleeves give this sweater a lovely relaxed fit.

feather and cloud

Sizes

XS (S, M, L, XL, XXL)

Finished chest circumference: 30 (34, 38, 42, 46, 50)" [75 (85, 95, 105, 115, 125) cm]. Choose a size with no ease.

Materials

Yarn: 4 (5, 5, 6, 7, 7) skeins of Tosh Chunky by Madelinetosh (100% merino wool; 165 yd [151 m] - 115 g). Approx. 650 (730, 820, 900, 1050, 1150) yd [600 (670, 750, 830, 960, 1050) m] of aran weight yarn. Sample is knit in colorway Esoteric, in size medium.

Needles: US 9 [5.5 mm] and US 8 [5 mm] circular needle, 32" [80 cm] long, and dpns. Adjust needle size if necessary to obtain the correct gauge.

Other: Tapestry needle, stitch markers, stitch holders or waste yarn and blocking aids.

Gauge

16 sts and 24 rows = 4" [10 cm] in reverse Stockinette stitch using larger needles.

Finished Size

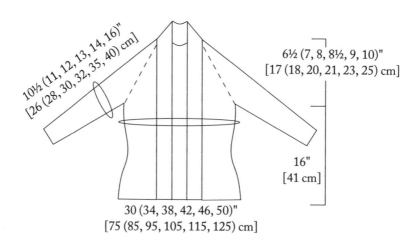

10½ (11, 12, 13, 14, 16)" [26 (28, 30, 32, 35, 40) cm]

6½ (7, 8, 8½, 9, 10)" [17 (18, 20, 21, 23, 25) cm]

16" [41 cm]

30 (34, 38, 42, 46, 50)" [75 (85, 95, 105, 115, 125) cm]

feather and cloud

Yoke

Using larger circular needle, CO 52 (56, 60, 64, 68, 68) sts. Work back and forth in reverse Stockinette stitch and begin raglan shaping. Knit one row (WS).

Row 1 (RS): p1, yo, pm, p1, yo, p8, yo, p1, pm, yo, p 30 (34, 38, 42, 46, 46), yo, pm, p1, yo, p8, yo, p1, pm, yo, p1.

Row 2 (WS): knit all sts.

Row 3 (RS): *p to m, yo, sm, p1, yo, p until 1 st before m remains, yo, p1, sm, yo; repeat once from *, p to end.

Row 4 (WS): knit all sts.

Repeat **rows 3 and 4** — 13 (15, 17, 19, 21, 25) times more [*172 (192, 212, 232, 252, 284) sts on needle*].

Divide for body and sleeves

(RS): *p to m, remove marker, place all sts before next marker on holder, sm; repeat once from *, p to end.

You have 92 (104, 116, 128, 140, 156) sts on needle for the body and 40 (44, 48, 52, 56, 64) sts on each holder for sleeves.

Body

Continue in reverse Stockinette stitch. When the body measures 3" [8 cm] from underarm, begin waist shaping.

Decrease row (RS): *p until 5 sts before m remain, p3tog, yo, p2, sm, p2, yo, sssp; repeat once from *, p to end.

Repeat the **decrease row** — 3 more times every 4th row [*16 sts decreased; 76 (88, 100, 112, 124, 140) sts on needle*]. Work 2" [5 cm] in reverse Stockinette stitch. Begin waist increases.

Increase row (RS): *p until 2 sts before m remain, yo, p2, sm, p2, yo; repeat once from *, p to end.

Repeat the **increase row** — 3 more times every 6th row [*16 sts increased; 92 (104, 116, 128, 140, 156) sts on needle*]. Work in reverse Stockinette stitch until the body measures 14½" [37 cm] from underarm. Change to smaller circular needle and work 1½" [4 cm] in 1X1-ribbing (*k1, p1; rep from * to end). BO sts loosely in ribbing.

Sleeves

Place sleeve sts from holder on dpns. Re-attach yarn, place marker for beginning of round and join. Work in reverse Stockinette stitch until sleeve measures 4" [10 cm] from underarm.

Decrease round: p2, ssp, p until 4 sts remain, p2tog, p2.

Repeat the **decrease round** three more times every 2" [5 cm]. Work in reverse Stockinette stitch until sleeve measures 12½" [32 cm] from underarm. Change to smaller dpns and work 1½" [4 cm] in 1X1- ribbing. BO sleeve sts loosely in ribbing.

Collar and front bands

Using larger circular needle and with RS of the work facing, pick up and knit 198 (216, 216, 234, 252, 270) sts evenly along the front and collar edges. Begin from the bottom of the right front edge. Knit the next row (WS). Work in garter stitch feather and fan pattern as follows:

Row 1 (RS): *[k2tog] 3 times, [yo, k1] 6 times, [k2tog] 3 times; repeat from * to end.

Row 2 (WS): k to end.

Repeat **rows 1 and 2** until the collar and front band measures 4" [10 cm] slightly stretched. BO sts on next RS row.

Finishing

Weave in all yarn ends. Block the cardigan using your preferred method.

rhythmic

We each move to the beat of our own drums in life, timing is what differentiates each of us. Rhythm gives us a sense of security, knowing what will come next because it has happened before. But all is not known and what comes next is only a guess.

Rhythm is the pulse in our lives, it is what keeps our pace, and drives us forward. May you find solace in the rhythm set by these designs.

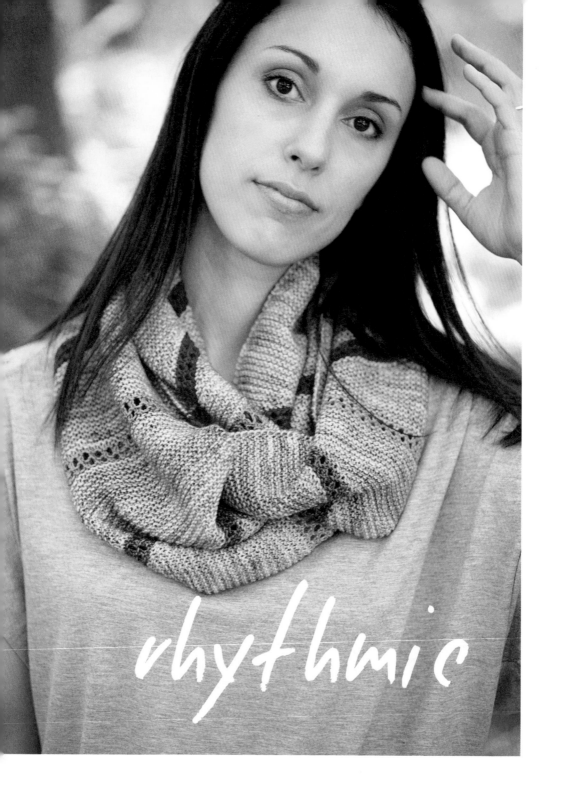

rhythmic

fine tune cowl

make space cardigan

fine tune

by joji locatelli

Brightly colored stripes rhythmically added to this simple but striking accessory. Fine Tune is worked lengthwise, in garter stitch, using short rows. Choose your main yarn color and your favorite leftovers for this, since you will only need a few yards of each contrasting color.

fine tune

Sizes

One size.
Finished measurements: 10½" [26 cm] wide and 57½" [144 cm] long loop.

Materials

Yarn: MC — 2 skeins of Merino Fingering by French Market Fibers (100% merino; 400 yd [363 m] - 100 g). Approx. 650 yd [595 m]. Shown in colorway On the Ghost Tour.

CC — You will need approx. 200 yd [183 m] of CC, divided into 4 colors. Shown in: CC1 (pink): Malabrigo Sock – Light of Love. CC2 (teal): Merino Lace by The Uncommon Thread (doubled) – Pontus. CC3 (yellow): BFL Sock by The Uncommon Thread – Golden Praline. CC4 (charcoal): BFL Sock by Lioness Arts - Hortense.

Needles: US 4 [3.5 mm] needles. Adjust needle size if necessary to obtain the correct gauge.

Other: Crochet hook, waste yarn, tapestry needle.

Gauge

23 stitches and 40 rows = 4" [10 cm] in garter stitch. *Note: Gauge is not crucial for this project. However, changes might result in a different yardage requirement.*

Finished Size

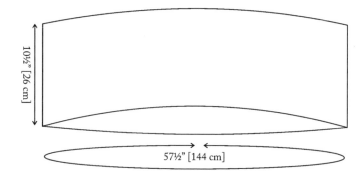

10½" [26 cm]

57½" [144 cm]

fine tune

Directions

With crochet hook and waste yarn, provisionally CO 61 st (see Glossary).

Start Pattern

With MC, knit 1 row.

> **Next row (WS):** Sl1, k to end.
> **Row 1:** Sl1, k1, W&T.
> **Row 2:** K to end.
> **Row 3:** Sl1, k to wrapped st, knit it (no need to lift the wrap), k1, W&T.
> **Row 4:** K to end.

Repeat **rows 3 and 4** until all st have been used up.

Switch to CC1.

Work EYELET BAND.

> **Row 1 (RS):** Knit to end.
> **Rows 2, 4 and 6 (WS):** Sl1, k to end.
> **Row 3:** Sl1, k1, *yo, k2tog* to 1 st from end, k1.
> **Row 5:** Sl1, k2, *yo, k2tog* to 2 st from end, k2.

Switch to MC.

> **Row 1 (RS):** K to 3 st before the end of row, W&T.
> **Row 2 (WS):** K to end.
> **Row 3:** Sl1, k to 2 st before previous wrap, W&T.
> **Row 4:** K to end.

Repeat **rows 3 and 4** until all st have been used up.

> **Next 2 rows (RS and WS):** Sl1, k to end.

Switch to CC2.

Work EYELET BAND (same as you did with CC1).

Switch to MC. Knit 1 row.

> **Row 1 (WS):** Sl1, k1, W&T.

> **Row 2 (RS):** K to end.
> **Row 3:** Sl1, k to wrapped st, knit it, k1, W&T.
> **Row 4:** K to end.

Repeat **rows 3 and 4** until all st have been used up.

> **Next row (WS):** Sl1, k to end.

Switch to CC3.

Work EYELET BAND.

Switch to MC. Knit 1 row.

> **Row 1 (WS):** Sl1, k to 3 st before the end of row, W&T.
> **Row 2 (RS):** K to end.
> **Row 3:** Sl1, k to 2 st before previous wrap, W&T.
> **Row 4:** K to end.

Repeat **rows 3 and 4** until all st have been used up.

> **Next row (WS):** Sl1, k to end.

Switch to CC4.

Work EYELET BAND.

Repeat instructions from "**Start Pattern**" 3 more times (4 repeats total). Do not bind off your st.

Finishing

Unravel the provisionally CO st and graft them together with the end row of your work. Make sure not to twist it.

make space

by veera välimäki

Make Space is truly a rhythmic cardigan. You can find a rhythm in shape, seeing how the yoke steadily grows and then continues with a different pace down to the accented stripe details. The cardigan has a lovely snug fit and features an eyelet yoke with some stripes and garter stitch details. It's worked in one piece from top down.

make space

Sizes

XS (S, M, L, XL, XXL)
Finished chest circumference: 30 (34, 38, 42, 46, 50)" [75 (85, 95, 105, 115, 125) cm].
Choose a size with no ease.

Materials

Yarn: 4 (5, 5, 6, 7, 8) skeins of Tosh Sport by Madelinetosh (100% merino wool; 270 yd [247 m] - 100 g); 3 (4, 4, 5, 6, 7) skeins in MC and 1 skein in CC. Approx. 980 (1100, 1250, 1360, 1480, 1600) yd [900 (1000, 1140, 1250, 1350, 1460) m] of sport weight yarn, both colors included. Sample is knit in colorways Tern (gray, MC) and Candlewick (yellow, CC), in size small.

Needles: US 6 [4 mm] and US 4 [3.5 mm] circular needle and dpns. Adjust needle size if necessary to obtain the correct gauge.

Other: Seven 1" [2.5 cm] buttons, tapestry needle, stitch markers, stitch holders / waste yarn and blocking aids.

Gauge

20 sts and 32 rows = 4" [10 cm] in Stockinette stitch, using larger needle.

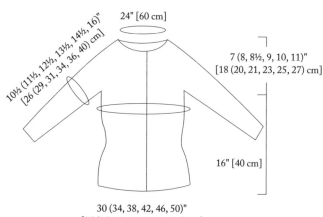

24" [60 cm]

10½ (11½, 12½, 13½, 14½, 16)" [26 (29, 31, 34, 36, 40) cm]

7 (8, 8½, 9, 10, 11)" [18 (20, 21, 23, 25, 27) cm]

16" [40 cm]

30 (34, 38, 42, 46, 50)" [75 (85, 95, 105, 115, 125) cm]

make

space

Collar

Using smaller circular needle and MC, CO 130 sts. Work back and forth in garter st until the piece measures ½" [1 cm]. Shape the neck with short rows.

> **Set-up short rows (RS and WS):** k until 40 sts remain, W&T.
>
> **Short rows 1 and 2 (RS and WS):** k 3 sts past previous wrapped st, W&T.

Work short **rows 1 and 2** five more times. Knit to end on next row. *Note: do not pick up the wraps, they will blend in garter stitche nicely.* Continue in garter stitch until the collar measures 1" [2.5 cm] at front.

Work the first buttonhole on next RS row (*instructions are for one-row buttonhole, you can work k2tog, yo –buttonhole if desired*): Work as established until 6 stitches remain, bring working yarn to front, slip the next stitch purlwise to right needle and bring yarn to back. *Slip the next st to right needle and pass the first slipped st over the second; repeat once from *. Turn work. Cast on 3 stitches using cable cast-on method (WS) and turn work again. Slip the next stitch on right needle and pass the last CO stitch over the slipped stitch, knit to end.

Continue in garter stitch until the collar measures 2" [5 cm] at front.

Yoke

Change to larger circular needle and continue in MC. Begin eyelet yoke with chart A and **at the same time** work buttonholes as established on collar every 2" [5 cm].

> **Set-up row (RS):** Work 10 sts in garter st, k5, work row 1 of chart A ten times, k5, work to end in garter st.
>
> **Set-up row (WS):** Work 10 sts in garter st, p5, work row 2 of chart A ten times, p5, work to end in garter st.
>
> **Row 1 (RS):** Work 10 sts in garter st, k5, work the next row of chart A ten times, k5, work to end in garter st.
>
> **Row 2 (WS):** Work 10 sts in garter st, p5, work the next row of chart A ten times, p5, work to end in garter st.

Repeat **rows 1 and 2**, working 4 (5, 6, 7, 8, 9) times through rows 5-10 of chart A and once through rows 11-16 of chart A [*250 (270, 290, 310, 330, 350 sts on needle*]. *Note: the rows 1–4 and rows 11-16 of the chart A are worked only once. You will have one more stitch on each edge of the chart after each repeat of rows 5 to 10.*

Divide for body and sleeves

> **(RS):** knit 41 (45, 49, 52, 56, 59) sts, place the next 48 (51, 53, 56, 58, 62) sts before next marker on holder, CO 2 (3, 4, 6, 7, 9) sts using cable cast-on method, pm, CO 1 (3, 4, 5, 6, 8) using cable cast-on method, k72 (78, 86, 94, 102, 108) sts, place the next 48 (51, 53, 56, 58, 62) sts before next marker on holder, CO 1 (3, 4, 5, 6, 8) sts using cable cast-on method, pm, CO 2 (3, 4, 6, 7, 9) using cable cast-on method, k41 (45, 49, 52, 56, 59) sts to end.

You have 160 (180, 200, 220, 240, 260) sts on needle for the body and 48 (51, 53, 56, 58, 62) sts on each holder for sleeves.

Body

Continue in MC and in Stockinette stitch, working 10-stitch garter stitch buttonbands on each end as established. Work a buttonhole as established every 2" [5 cm] until all seven buttonholes are worked. When the body measures 3" [8 cm] from underarm, begin waist shaping.

> **Decrease row (RS):** *k until 8 sts before m remain, k2tog, k to m, sm, k6, ssk; repeat once from *, k to end.

Chart A

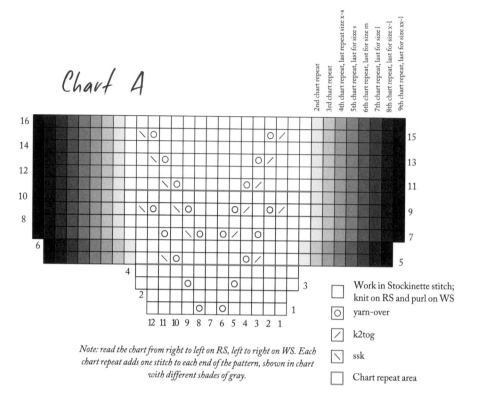

Note: read the chart from right to left on RS, left to right on WS. Each chart repeat adds one stitch to each end of the pattern, shown in chart with different shades of gray.

Legend:
- ☐ Work in Stockinette stitch; knit on RS and purl on WS
- Ⓞ yarn-over
- ╱ k2tog
- ╲ ssk
- ☐ Chart repeat area

Repeat the *decrease row* 3 more times every 4th row [*16 sts decreased; 144 (164, 184, 204, 224, 244) sts on needle*]. Work 2" [5 cm] in St st and buttonbands. Begin waist increases.

Increase row (RS): *k until 7 sts before m remain, m1L, k to m, sm, k 7, m1R; repeat once from *, k to end.

Repeat the *increase row* 3 more times every 6th row [*16 sts increased; 160 (180, 200, 220, 240, 260) sts on needle*] **and at the same time**, after the second increase row, add CC striping beginning on a RS row: work 2 rounds in CC and 2 rounds in MC. Work striping in Stockinette stitch until the body measures 13" [33 cm] from underarm. Change to smaller circular needle and continue in garter st until the body measures 16" [40 cm] from underarm. BO body sts loosely.

Sleeves

Place 48 (51, 53, 56, 58, 62) sleeve sts from holder on larger dpns. Re-attach MC yarn and pick up and knit 2 (3, 4, 6, 7, 9) from middle of the underarm, knit stitches from dpn and pick up and knit 2 (4, 5, 6, 7, 9) sts to middle of the underarm. Place a marker for beginning of round. Work in Stockinette stitch until sleeve measures 4" [10 cm] from underarm.

Decrease round: k4, ssk, k until 6 sts remain, k2tog, k to end.

Repeat the *decrease round* twice every 2" [5 cm] **and at the same time,** when sleeve measures 6" [15 cm] from underarm, add CC striping: work 2 rounds in CC and 2 rounds in MC. Work striping in Stockinette stitch until sleeve measures 17" [42 cm] from underarm. Change to smaller dpns and continue in garter st until sleeve measures 20" [50 cm] from underarm. BO sleeve sts loosely.

Finishing

Weave in all yarn ends. Sew buttons to left front. Block the cardigan using your preferred method.

reflection

To see your image reflected back in a pool of water on a glowing day is Mother Nature's magic. Her ultimate compliment is to share back with you the beauty she sees.

In these designs we pay homage to the simple things that we see in nature, reflecting back to her what we see. It is this inspiration that has set these designs in motion.

reflection

at dawn shawl

fathom beanie

39

at dawn
by joji locatelli

Reflected lines and perspective take the center stage in this asymmetrical shawl. Short rows, garter stitch and stripes... A well-known combination for an enjoyable knit.

at dawn

Sizes

Finished measurements: 80" [200 cm] from side to side and 26" [65 cm] from top to bottom at deepest point.

Materials

Yarn: You will need 2 colors of fingering weight yarn.

Main Color (MC): 1 skein of BFL Sock by The Uncommon Thread (100% wool; 437 yd [399m] - 100 g) Shown in colorway Golden Praline.

Contrasting Color (CC): 1 skein of Posh Fingering by The Uncommon Thread (70% wool, 20% silk, 10% cashmere; 440 yd [402 m] - 100 g) Shown in colorway Brassica. *Note: the whole skein of CC is needed!*

Needles: US 2½ [3 mm] circular or straight needles.

Other: Row counter, darning needle for weaving in ends, blocking wires.

Gauge

20 stitches and 30 rows = 4" [10 cm] in garter stitch, after blocking (really stretching the fabric). *Note: Gauge is not crucial for this project. However, changes might result in a different yardage requirement.*

Finished Measurements

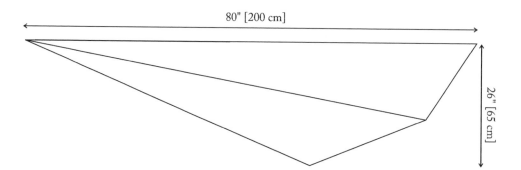

80" [200 cm]

26" [65 cm]

at dawn

Bottom Half

Using MC, CO 254 st.

> *Set-up row:* K to end.

MC Stripe 1

> *Row 1:* Sl1, k1, m1R, k to 4 st from end, wrap next st and turn (W&T).
>
> *Row 2 and all foll WS rows:* K to end.
>
> *Row 3:* Sl1, k to 4 st from last wrapped st (you should have on your left needle: 4 "free" st, then the last wrapped st, and then the rest of the stitches of the row. The next stitch you will wrap is the first of these 4 "free" st), W&T.
>
> *Row 5:* Sl1, k1, m1R, k to 4 st from last wrapped st, W&T.

Work *rows 3-6* six more times, (you should have worked 30 rows in garter stitch in MC).

CC Stripe

Switch to CC.

> *Row 1:* K to 4 st before last wrapped st, W&T.
>
> *Row 2:* K to end.

MC Stripe 2

Switch to MC.

> *Row 1:* Sl1, k1, m1R, k to 4 st before last wrapped st, W&T.
>
> *Row 2 and all foll WS rows:* K to end.
>
> *Row 3:* Sl1, k to 4 st before last wrapped st, W&T.

Work *rows 1-4* five more times, and then rows 1-2 once more (you should have worked 26 rows in garter stitch in MC).

Work a CC Stripe.

MC Stripe 3: Work rows 1-4 as for MC stripe 2 five times, and then rows 1-2 once more (you should have worked 22 rows in garter stitch in MC).

Work a CC Stripe.

MC Stripe 4: Work rows 1-4 as for MC stripe 2 four times, and then rows 1-2 once more (you should have worked 18 rows in garter stitch in MC).

Work a CC Stripe.

MC Stripe 5: Work rows 1-4 as for MC stripe 2 three times, and then rows 1-2 once more (you should have worked 14 rows in garter stitch in MC).

Work a CC Stripe.

MC Stripe 6: Work rows 1-4 as for MC stripe 2 twice, and then rows 1-2 once more (you should have worked 10 rows in garter stitch in MC).

Work a CC Stripe.

MC Stripe 7: Work rows 1-4 as for MC stripe 2 once, and then rows 1-2 once more (you should have worked 6 rows in garter stitch in MC).

Work a CC Stripe.

Switch to MC.

Next row (RS): Sl1, k1, m1R, k to 4 st from last wrapped st, W&T.

Next row (WS): K to end.

Next row: Sl1, k to the end of row, without picking up wraps.

Next row: Sl1, k to end.

Top half

Switch to CC.

Row 1 (RS): K1, m1R, k to the end of row.

Row 2 (WS): Sl1, k to the end of row.

Row 3: Sl1, k2, W&T.

Row 4: K to end

Row 5: Sl1, k1, m1R, knit to last wrapped st, knit it, k3, W&T.

Row 6: K to end.

MC Stripe

Switch to MC.

Row 1: K to last wrapped st, knit it, k3, W&T.

Row 2: K to end.

CC Stripe 1

Switch to CC

Row 1: Sl1, k1, m1R, k to last wrapped st, knit it, k3, W&T.

Row 2 and all foll WS rows: K to the end of row.

Row 3: Sl1, k to last wrapped st, knit it, k3, W&T.

Work row 4 once, and then another row 1 and 2 (you should have worked 6 rows in garter stitch in CC).

Work a MC Stripe.

CC Stripe 2: Work rows 1-4 as for CC stripe 1 twice, and then rows 1-2 once more (you should have worked 10 rows in garter stitch in CC).

Work a MC Stripe.

CC Stripe 3: Work rows 1-4 as for CC stripe 1 three times, and then rows 1-2 once more (you should have worked 14 rows in garter stitch in CC).

Work a MC Stripe.

CC Stripe 4: Work rows 1-4 as for CC stripe 1 four times, and then rows 1-2 once more (you should have worked 18 rows in garter stitch in CC).

Work a MC Stripe.

CC Stripe 5: Work rows 1-4 as for CC stripe 1 five times, and then rows 1-2 once more (you should have worked 22 rows in garter stitch in CC).

Work a MC Stripe.

CC Stripe 6: Work rows 1-4 as for CC stripe 1 six times, and then rows 1-2 once more (you should have worked 26 rows in garter stitch in CC).

Work a MC Stripe.

CC Stripe 7: Work rows 1-4 as for CC stripe 1 seven times, and then rows 1-2 once more (you should have worked 30 rows in garter stitch in CC).

With CC, knit to the end of row.

On the next row, bind off all st loosely.

Finishing

Weave in ends and block shawl to measurements.

fathom

by veera välimäki

Fathom is a lovely beanie with a small amount of slouch, keeping you both stylish and warm. Echoes of the cables, blended with squishy stitch pattern, make this piece a balanced combination for an interesting and quick knit!

Sizes

One size.

Finished brim circumference: 19" [48 cm]
Finished body circumference: 20¾" [52 cm]

Materials

Yarn: 1 skein of Primo Sport by The Plucky Knitter (75% merino wool, 20% cashmere, 5% nylon; 275 yd [250 m] - 100 g). Approx. 225 yd [200 m] of sport weight yarn. Sample is knit in colorway Lonesome Highway.

Needles: US 2½ [3 mm] and US 4 [3.5 mm] circular needle, 16" [40 cm] long, and larger dpns. Adjust needle size if necessary to obtain the correct gauge.

Other: Cable needle (CN), tapestry needle, stitch markers and blocking aids.

Gauge

22 sts and 38 rows = 4" [10 cm] in texture stitch, using larger needles.

Finished Size

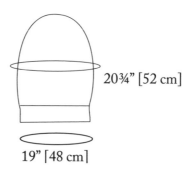

20¾" [52 cm]

19" [48 cm]

fathom

Stitch patterns

Twisted ribbing
In the round - *k1 tbl, p1; repeat from * to end of round.

Texture stitch
Multiple of 2 stitches and 4 rounds.
Round 1: Knit all stitches.
Round 2: *k1, p1; repeat from * to end of round.
Round 3: Purl all stitches.
Round 4: *p1, k1; repeat from * to end of round.

Brim

Using smaller circular needle, CO 106 sts. Place marker for beginning of round and carefully join without twisting your stitches. Work in twisted 1X1 ribbing until the brim measures 1½" [4 cm].

Body

Change to larger circular needle and continue in stitch pattern and cable and increase on first round.
Set-up round (increase round): Sm, work the first row of chart A (21 stitches), pm, m1R, *work 10 sts in texture stitch (round 1: knit), m1R, work 11 sts in texture stitch (knit), m1R; repeat four times from *, k1. [*115 sts on needle*].
Round 1: Sm, work the next row of chart A, sm, work to end of round in next round of texture stitch.

Repeat **round 1**, working across all rows of chart A, until the beanie measures 7" [18 cm] from the cast-on edge, ending with round 4 of the texture stitch.

Crown decreases

Begin crown decreases on next round.

Round 2 (first decrease round): Sm, work the next row of chart A, sm, *ssk, k12, k2tog, pm, ssk, k11, k2tog, pm, ssk, k12, k2tog, pm; repeat once from *.
Round 3: Sm, work the next row of chart A, sm, work in stitch pattern to end of round slipping markers (*note: work the stitch pattern continuously, starting with the stitch that previously was the second stitch*).
Round 4 (decrease round): Sm, work the next row of chart A, sm, *ssp, p until 2 sts before m remain, p2tog, sm; repeat from * 5 times more.
Round 5: Sm, work the next row of chart A, sm, work in stitch pattern to end of round slipping markers (*note: work the stitch pattern continuously, starting with the stitch that previously was the second stitch*).
Round 6 (decrease round): Sm, work the next row of chart A, sm, *ssk, k until 2 sts before m remain, k2tog, sm; repeat from * 5 times more.

Repeat the **rounds 3-6** once more.

Round 7: Sm, p2tog, k2tog four times (cable stitches), p2tog, k1 tbl, p2tog, k2tog twice, p2tog, sm, work in stitch pattern to end of round slipping markers (*note: work the stitch pattern continuously, starting with the stitch that previously was the second stitch*).

Cut yarn and thread through remaining stitches twice. Fasten off securely.

Finishing

Weave in all yarn ends. Block the beanie using your preferred method.

Chart A

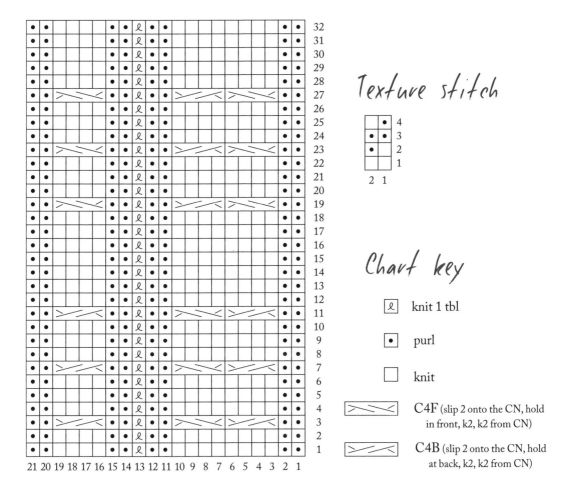

Texture stitch

Chart key

ℓ   knit 1 tbl

•   purl

☐   knit

C4F (slip 2 onto the CN, hold in front, k2, k2 from CN)

C4B (slip 2 onto the CN, hold at back, k2, k2 from CN)

crisp

It's that moment when you step outside and you feel the cold air envelope you. The sound you hear is the crunching of icy leaves beneath your feet. That biting feeling that catches your breath and you exhale and see it.
The crisp cold air beckons you to walk with an added spring to your step, just a little faster as if you were a few years younger. Your heart beats quickly and in this moment you feel alive, youthful and at full attention!

crisp

see you there cardigan

dipped cowl

see you there
by joji locatelli

Small, easy cables and carefully shaped silhouette make this hoodie a pleasure to knit and wear. This cozy cardigan is worked seamlessly from the top down using the contiguous method, which makes finishing easy and fast. Whether you choose a calming neutral hue for a classic look, or a bright bold color for a statement piece, this will be your chilly weather staple.

see you there

Sizes

To fit bust: 28 (30/32, 34/36, 38/40, 42/44, 46/48, 50/52, 54/56)" [70 (75/80, 85/90, 95/100, 105/110, 115/120, 125/130, 135/140) cm]. Shown in size 34/36. *Note: See more detailed finished measurements below in schematics picture or written on page 63.*

Materials

Yarn: 5 (6, 7, 7, 8, 9, 9, 10) skeins of Worsted MCN by Madelinetosh (80% merino, 10% cashmere,10% nylon; 187 yd [171 m] - 100 g). Shown in colorway Antler.
Needles: US 7 [4.5 mm] and US 6 [4 mm] circular needles.
Other: 9 (9, 9, 9, 10, 10, 10, 10) 5/8" [15 mm] buttons, cable needle, stitch markers, waste yarn or stitch holders.

Gauge

17 st and 24 rows = 4" [10 cm] on US 7 [4.5 mm] needles, in Stockinette stitch, after blocking.

Finished Measurements

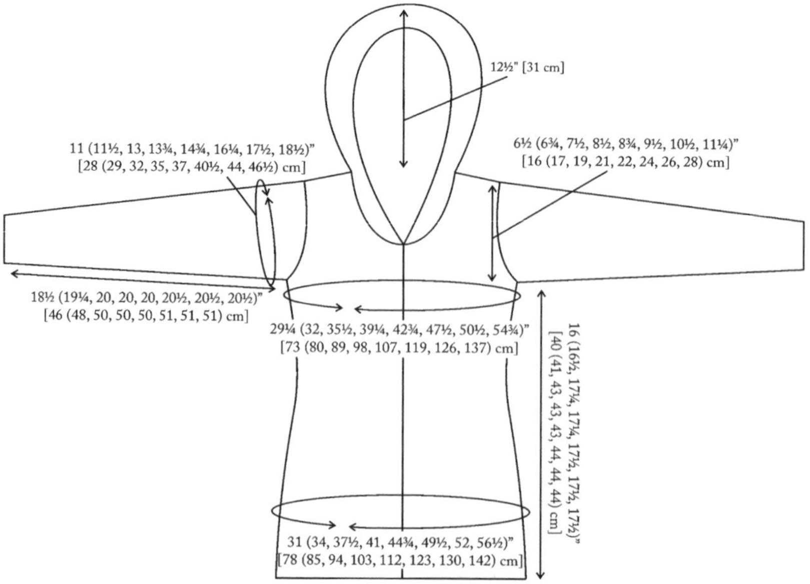

12½" [31 cm]
11 (11½, 13, 13¾, 14¾, 16¼, 17½, 18½)" [28 (29, 32, 35, 37, 40½, 44, 46½) cm]
6½ (6¾, 7½, 8½, 8¾, 9½, 10½, 11¼)" [16 (17, 19, 21, 22, 24, 26, 28) cm]
18½ (19¼, 20, 20, 20, 20½, 20½, 20½)" [46 (48, 50, 50, 50, 51, 51, 51) cm]
29¼ (32, 35½, 39¼, 42¾, 47½, 50½, 54¾)" [73 (80, 89, 98, 107, 119, 126, 137) cm]
16 (16½, 17¼, 17¼, 17½, 17½, 17½)" [40 (41, 43, 43, 43, 44, 44, 44) cm]
31 (34, 37½, 41, 44¾, 49½, 52, 56½)" [78 (85, 94, 103, 112, 123, 130, 142) cm]

see you there

Stitches Used

Mini Cable Back (MCB)

Worked flat –

> **Row 1:** K2
> **Rows 2 and 4:** P2
> **Row 3:** C2B (see Abbreviations).

Repeat these 4 rows.

Worked in the round –

> **Rounds 1, 2, 4:** K2
> **Round 3:** C2B.

Repeat these 4 rounds.

Mini Cable Front (MCF)

Worked flat –

> **Row 1:** K2
> **Rows 2 and 4:** P2
> **Row 3:** C2F (see Abbreviations).

Repeat these 4 rows.

Worked in the round –

> **Rounds 1, 2, 4:** K2
> **Round 3:** C2F.

Repeat these 4 rounds.

Mini Cable Panel (MCP)

(Worked over a multiple of 4 + 2 st)

> **Row 1:** Knit all st.
> **All even rows:** Purl all st.
> **Row 3:** C2F (see Abbreviations), (C2B, C2F) to end.
> **Row 5:** Knit all st.
> **Row 7:** C2B, (C2F, C2B) to end.

Repeat these 8 rows.

Cable A *(worked over 6 st)*

> **Rows 1 and 5:** Knit.
> **All even rows:** Purl
> **Row 3:** C6B (see Abbreviations).

Repeat these 6 rows.

Cable B *(worked over 6 st)*

> **Rows 1 and 5:** Knit.
> **All even rows:** Purl
> **Row 3:** C6F (see Abbreviations).

Repeat these 6 rows.

Directions

Setting up the cables and contiguous pattern

Using US 7 (4.5 mm) needles, CO 36 (40, 40, 40, 44, 44, 44, 44) st.

> **Set-up row:** K1, pm, k1, p2, k1, pm, k2, p22 (26, 26, 26, 30, 30, 30, 30), k2, pm, k1, p2, k1, pm, k1.
> **Row 1 (RS):** P1, m1R, sm, p1, MCB (see Stitches Used), p1, sm, m1L, p2, work Mini Cable Panel (MCP) over 22 (26, 26, 26, 30, 30, 30, 30) st, p2, m1R, sm, p1, MCF, p1, sm, m1L, p1.
> **Row 2 (WS):** K1, p1, m1Lp, sm, k1, MCF, k1, sm, m1Rp, p1, k2, MCP, k2, p1, m1Lp, sm, k1, MCB, k1, sm, m1Rp, p1, k1. *44 (48, 48, 48, 52, 52, 52, 52) st.*
> **Row 3:** P1, k2, m1R, sm, p1, MCB, p1, sm, m1L, k2, p2, MCP, p2, k2, m1R, sm, p1, MCF, p1, sm, m1L, k2, p1.
> **Row 4:** K1, p3, m1Lp, sm, k1, MCF, k1, sm, m1Rp, p3, k2, MCP, k2, p3, m1Lp, sm, k1, MCB, k1, sm, m1Rp, p3, k1. *52 (56, 56, 56, 60, 60, 60, 60) st.*
> **Row 5:** P1, k4, m1R, sm, p1, MCB, p1, sm, m1L, k4, p2, MCP, p2, k4, m1R, sm, p1, MCF, p1, sm, m1L, k4, p1.
> **Row 6:** K1, p5, m1Lp, sm, k1, MCF, k1, sm, m1Rp, p5, k2, MCP, k2, p5, m1Lp, sm, k1, MCB, k1, sm, m1Rp, p5, k1. *60 (64, 64, 64, 68, 68, 68, 68) st.*
> **Row 7:** p1, k6, m1Rp, sm, p1, MCB, p1, sm, m1Lp, K6, p2, MCP, p2, k6, m1Rp, sm, p1, MCF, p1, sm, m1Lp, k6, p1.
> **Row 8:** K1, p6, k1, m1L, sm, k1, MCF, k1, sm, m1R, k1, p6, k2, MCP, k2, p6, k1, m1L, sm, k1, MCB, k1, sm, m1R, k1, p6, k1. *68 (72, 72, 72,*

76, 76, 76, 76) st.

Row 9: P1, work Cable A (see Stitches Used), p2, m1R, sm, p1, MCB, p1, sm, m1L, p2, work Cable B, p2, MCP, p2, work Cable A, p2, m1R, sm, p1, MCF, p1, sm, m1L, p2, Cable B, p1.

Row 10: K1, Cable B, K2, p1, m1Lp, sm, k1, MCF, k1, sm, m1Rp, p1, k2, Cable A, k2, MCP, k2, Cable B, k2, p1, m1Lp, sm, k1, MCB, k1, sm, m1Rp, p1, k2, Cable A, k1. *76 (80, 80, 80, 84, 84, 84, 84) st.*

Row 11: P1, Cable A, p2, pm, k to next m, m1R, sm, p1, MCB, p1, sm, m1L, k2, pm, p2, Cable B, p2, MCP, p2, Cable A, p2, pm, k to next m, m1R, sm, p1, MCF, p1, sm, m1L, k2, pm, p2, Cable B, p1.

Row 12: K1, Cable B, k2, sm, p to next m, m1Lp, sm, k1, MCF, k1, sm, m1Rp, p to next m, sm, k2, Cable A, k2, MCP, k2, Cable B, k2, sm, p to next m, m1Lp, sm, k1, MCB, k1, sm, m1Rp, p to next m, sm, k2, Cable A, k1. *84 (88, 88, 88, 92, 92, 92, 92) st.*

Row 13: p1, Cable A, p2, sm, k to next m, m1R, sm, p1, MCB, p1, sm, m1L, k to next m, sm, p2, Cable B, p2, MCP, p2, Cable A, p2, sm, k to next m, m1R, sm, p1, MCF, p1, sm, m1L, k to next m, sm, p2, Cable B, p1.

Row 14: Same as row 12.

Work *rows 13-14* — 1 (1, 1, 2, 2, 3, 3, 5) more times.

You should now have 100 (104, 104, 112, 116, 124, 124, 140) st: 58 (62, 62, 66, 70, 74, 74, 82) for the back, 17 (17, 17, 19, 19, 21, 21, 25) for each front and 4 for each shoulder slope.

Start sleeve and neck shaping

Note: On this row, it might be useful to place sleeve markers that have a different color, so you can differentiate them.

Row 1 (RS): P1, m1Lp, pm, Cable A, p2, sm, k to 1 st before marker, sl 1 to RN, remove marker, slip the stitch back to LN, place sleeve m (psm), m1R, k1, p1, MCB, p1, remove m, k1, m1L, psm, k to next m, sm, p2, Cable B, p2, MCP, p2, Cable A, p2, sm, K to 1 st before marker, sl 1 to RN, remove marker, slip the stitch back to LN, psm, m1R, k1, p1, MCF, p1, remove m, k1, m1L, psm, k to next m, sm, p2, Cable B, pm, m1Rp, p1.

Row 2 (WS): K to 1st m, sm, Cable B, k2, sm,

p to next m, sm, m1Lp, p2, k1, MCF, k1, p2, m1Rp, sm, work in established pattern to next sleeve marker, sm, m1Lp, p2, k1, MCB, k1, p2, m1Rp, sm, p to next m, sm, k2, Cable A, sm, k to end.

You should now have 110 (114, 114, 122, 126, 134, 134, 150) st: 56 (60, 60, 64, 68, 72, 82, 80) for the back, 17 (17, 17, 19, 19, 21, 21, 25) for each front and 10 for each sleeve.

Row 3: P1, m1Lp, work in the established pattern to first sleeve marker, sm, m1R, work in the established patt to next marker, m1L, sm, work across back in the established pattern until next sleeve marker, sm, m1R, work in patt to next marker, m1L, sm, work in patt to 1 st before the end, m1Rp, p1. 6 st increased.

Row 4: Work in the established pattern (knitting st as they appear) to 1st sleeve marker, sm, m1Lp, work in patt to next m, m1Rp, sm, work in established pattern to next sleeve marker, sm, m1Lp, work in patt to next m, m1Rp, sm, work in patt to end. 4 st increased.

Row 5: K1, m1L, work in the established pattern to first sleeve marker, sm, m1R, work in the established patt to next marker, m1L, sm, work across back in the established pattern until next sleeve marker, sm, m1R, work in patt to next marker, m1L, sm, work in patt to 1 st before the end, m1R, k1. 6 st increased.

Row 6: Work all st in pattern (as they appear) without increasing any stitches on this row.

You should now have 126 (130, 130, 138, 142, 150, 150, 166) st: 56 (60, 60, 64, 68, 72, 72, 80) for the back, 19 (19, 19, 21, 21, 23, 23, 27) for each front and 16 for each sleeve.

Work *rows 5-6* — 2 (3, 3, 5, 5, 6, 6, 7) more times.

You should now have a total of 138 (148, 148, 168, 172, 186, 186, 208): 56 (60, 60, 64, 68, 72, 72, 80) for the back, 21 (22, 22, 26, 26, 29, 29, 34) for each front and 20 (22, 22, 26, 26, 28, 28, 30) for each sleeve.

Next row (RS): CO 8 (9, 9, 7, 9, 8, 8, 7), p3 (2, 2, 2, 3, 3, 3, 3), k1, p2 (1, 1, 1, 2, 2, 2, 2), k6 (10, 10, 10, 10, 10, 10, 10), p2, sm, work in pattern to first sleeve marker, sm, m1R, work in patt to next marker, m1L, sm, work in pattern to next sleeve marker, sm, m1R, work in patt to next m, m1L, sm, work in patt to end.

Next row (WS): CO 8 (9, 9, 7, 9, 8, 8, 7), k3 (2, 2, 2, 3, 3, 3, 3), p1, k2 (1, 1, 1, 2, 2, 2, 2), p6 (10, 10, 10, 10, 10, 10, 10), k2, work in patt to 8 (9, 9, 7, 9, 8, 8, 7) st before the end of row, p2 (5, 5, 3, 3, 2, 2, 1), k2 (1, 1, 1, 2, 2, 2, 2), p1, k3 (2, 2, 2, 3, 3, 3, 3).

You should now have a total of 158 (170, 170, 186, 194, 206, 206, 226) st: 56 (60, 60, 64, 68, 72, 72, 80) for the back, 29 (31, 31, 33, 35, 37, 37, 41) for each front and 22 (24, 24, 28, 28, 30, 30, 32) for each sleeve.

Work more sleeve increases

Row 1 (RS): P3 (2, 2, 2, 3, 3, 3, 3), sl1 pwise wyb, p2 (1, 1, 1, 2, 2, 2, 2), work MCP over 6 (10, 10, 10, 10, 10, 10, 10) st -starting on the same row as your back MCP-, p2, work in patt to first sleeve m, sm, m1R, work in patt to next m, m1L, sm, work in patt to next sleeve m, sm, m1R, work in patt to next m, m1L, sm, work in patt to last 12 (14, 14, 14, 16, 16, 16) st, work MCP over 6 (10, 10, 10, 10, 10, 10, 10) st -starting on the 4th following row of the repeat so that the fronts are mirrored-, p2 (1, 1, 1, 2, 2, 2, 2), sl1 pwise wyb, p3 (2, 2, 2, 3, 3, 3, 3). 4 st increased.

Row 2 (WS): K3 (2, 2, 2, 3, 3, 3, 3), p1, k2 (1, 1, 1, 2, 2, 2, 2), MCP over 6 (10, 10, 10, 10, 10, 10, 10) st, work in patt to last 12 (14, 14, 14, 16, 16, 16, 16) st, MCP over 6 (10, 10, 10, 10, 10, 10, 10) st, k2 (1, 1, 1, 2, 2, 2, 2), p1, k3 (2, 2, 2, 3, 3, 3, 3).

Repeat these 2 rows — 8 (8, 8, 8, 9, 9, 9, 9) more times.

You should have now 40 (42, 42, 46, 48, 50, 50, 52) st for each sleeve.

Work rest of sleeve increases and armhole shaping

Row 1 (RS): Work in patt to 1 st before first sleeve m, m1L, k1 sm, m1R, work in patt to next m, m1L, sm, k1, m1R work in patt to 1 st before next sleeve m, m1L, k1, sm, m1R, work in patt to next m, m1L, sm, k1, m1R, work in patt to end of row.

Row 2 (WS): Work in patt to 1 st before first sleeve m, m1Rp, p1, sm, work sleeve st in patt without increases, sm, p1, m1Lp, work in patt to 1 st before next sleeve m, m1Rp, p1, sm, work sleeve st in patt without increases, sm, p1, m1Lp, work in patt to end of row.

Repeat these 2 rows — 0 (0, 1, 2, 2, 3, 5, 5) more times.

You should now have a total of 206 (218, 230, 258, 270, 294, 318, 338) st: 60 (64, 68, 76, 80, 88, 96, 104) st for the back, 31 (33, 35, 39, 41, 45, 49, 53) for each front and 42 (44, 46, 52, 54, 58, 62, 64) for each sleeve.

Divide for body and sleeves

Next row (RS): Work in patt to 1st sleeve marker, remove m, slip next 42 (44, 46, 52, 54, 58, 62, 64) st onto a piece of waste yarn, remove m, CO 1 (2, 4, 4, 6, 7, 6, 7), pm, CO 1, pm, CO 1 (2, 4, 4, 6, 7, 6, 7), work across all back st in patt, remove sleeve m, slip next 42 (44, 46, 52, 54, 58, 62, 64) st onto a piece of waste yarn, remove m, CO 1 (2, 4, 6, 7, 6, 7), pm, CO 1, pm, CO 1 (2, 4, 4, 6, 7, 6, 7), work in patt to end.

You should have a total of 128 (140, 156, 172, 188, 208, 220, 240): 62 (68, 76, 84, 92, 102, 108, 118) st for the back, 32 (35, 39, 43, 47, 52, 55, 60) st for each front and 1 st for each faux seam.

By this time, you sure can recognize how to work the fronts and back in pattern, so you can remove any markers that are not the "side seam" markers, to avoid confusion.

Body

Next row (WS): Work in patt to side seam marker, sm, k1, sm, work in patt to other seam marker, sm, k1, sm, work in patt to end.

Next row (RS): Work in patt to marker, sm, p1, sm, work in patt to next marker, sm, p1, sm, work in patt to end.

Continue working in the established pattern until work measures 4" [10 cm] from your armhole, ending on a WS row.

Next row (RS): Work in patt to 7 (8, 10, 12, 13, 15, 17, 19) st before marker, ssk, place dart marker, k1, k2tog, k to next m, sm, p1, sm, k3 (3, 5, 7, 8, 11, 12, 15), ssk, place dart marker, k1, k2tog, work in patt to 7 (8, 10, 12, 13, 15, 17, 19) st before next marker, ssk, place dart marker, k1, k2tog, k to next m, sm, p1, sm, k3 (3, 5, 7, 8, 11, 12, 15), ssk, place dart marker, k1, k2tog, work in patt to end.

Next row (WS): Work in patt to side seam marker, sm, k1, sm, work in patt to other seam marker, sm, k1, sm, work in patt to end. Work 6 more rows in patt.

On the foll row, work a waist decrease row: *Work in patt to 2 st before dart marker, ssk, sm, k1, k2tog* 4 times, work in patt to end of row.

Work 7 rows in patt, and then work a decrease row again. Work 7 more rows in patt.

On the foll row, work a waist increase row: *Work in patt to dart marker, m1R, sm, k1, m1L* 4 times, work in patt to end of row.

Continue working in pattern, repeating an increase row every 8th following row 3 more times.

You should have a total of 136 (148, 164, 180, 196, 216, 228, 248) st: 66 (72, 80, 88, 96, 106, 112, 122) st for the back, 34 (37, 41, 45, 49, 54, 57, 62) st for each front and 1 st for each faux seam.

When work measures 13½ (14, 14¾, 14¾, 14¾, 15¼, 15¼, 15¼)”; [34 (35, 37, 37, 37, 38, 38, 38) cm] from your armhole, switch to US 6 [4 mm] needles, and work bottom ribbing.

Sizes 28, 46/48 and 54/56

Set-up row (RS): K2, p1, p2tog, k2, *p2, k2* to 5 st before the end of row, p2tog, p1, k2.

Sizes 30/32, 34/36, 38/40, 42/44 and 50/52

Set-up row (RS): K2, p1, m1p, k2, *p2, k2* to 5 st before the end of row, m1p, p1, k2

All sizes:

Next and all foll WS rows: P2, (k2, p2) to the end of row.

Row 1 (RS): K2, p2, (C2B, p2, C2F, p2), to 2 st before the end of row, K2.

Row 3 (RS): K2, (p2, k2) to the end of row.

Repeat *rows 1-4* 2 more times, and then rows 1-2 once more. On the foll row (RS), BO all st in pattern.

Sleeves

Note: When working the sleeves in pattern, now you have to work the mini-cables in the round (see Stitches Used).

With US 7 [4.5 mm] needles, and starting at the center armhole, pick up and knit 1 st aligned with the faux seam st from the body, pick up and knit 2 (2, 4, 3, 4, 5, 6, 7) more st. Place the 42

(44, 46, 52, 54, 58, 62, 64) held stitches of a sleeve onto the left needle, work in pattern to end of round. Pick up and knit 2 (2, 4, 3, 4, 5, 6, 7) more stitches, reaching the center of the armhole again. Place marker.

You should have 47 (49, 55, 59, 63, 69, 75, 79) st.

Next round: P1, work in patt to end of round. Work 7 more rounds in the established pattern.

Next round – Decrease round: Work in pattern to 2 st before marker, k2tog, sm, p1, ssk. 2 st decreased.

Continue working in pattern and repeat a decrease round on the following 10th (10th, 8th, 8th, 8th, 6th, 4th, 4th) row 3 (3, 5, 7, 8, 10, 13, 14) more times. 39 (41, 43, 43, 45, 47, 47, 49) st remain.

When sleeve measures 14½ (15¼, 16, 16, 16, 16½, 16½, 16½)” [36 (38, 40, 40, 40, 41, 41, 41) cm] - or 4” [10 cm] before desired length - work cuff. Switch to US 6 [4 mm] needles.

Next round: K2tog, p1 *k1, p1*, repeat to the end of round.

Continue working in ribbing until sleeve measures 18½ (19¼, 20, 20, 20, 20½, 20½, 20½)” [46 (48, 50, 50, 50, 51, 51, 51) cm] from armhole or desired length.

Hood

With US 7 [4.5 mm] needles, pick up and knit 21 (23, 23, 25, 25, 27, 27, 27) st along the right front neckline, pick up 22 (26, 26, 26, 30, 30, 30, 30) st along the back neck and 21 (23, 23, 25, 25, 27, 27, 27) more along the left front. *64 (72, 72, 76, 80, 84, 84, 84) st.*

Set-up (WS): Purl to end.

Row 1 (RS): K3, wrap next st and turn (W&T - see Glossary).

Row 2: P to end.

Row 3: K to last wrapped st, knit it tog with wrap, k3, W&T.

Row 4: P to end.

Repeat the last 2 rows — 4 more times.

Row 13 (RS): K to end of row, picking up wrap as you find it and knitting it tog with its corresponding st.

Row 14 (WS): P3, W&T.

Row 15 (RS): K to end.

Row 16 (WS): P to last wrapped st, purl it tog with wrap, p3, W&T.

Row 17 (RS): K to end.

Repeat the last 2 rows — 4 more times.

Row 26 (WS): P to end of row, picking up wrap as you find it and purling it tog with its corresponding st.

Work 2 rows in Stockinette st.

Next row (RS): K31 (35, 35, 37, 39, 41, 41, 41), m1R, k1, pm, k1, m1L, k to end.

Work 5 rows in Stockinette st.

Next row: K to 1 st before m, m1R, k1, sm, k1, m1L, k to end.

Repeat the last 6 rows — 3 (3, 3, 3, 2, 2, 2, 2) more times. *74 (82, 82, 86, 88, 92, 92, 92) st.*

Continue working in Stockinette st until your hood measures 10½" [26 cm] measured along the center back, ending with a WS row.

Next row (RS): K to 3 st before m, k2tog, k1, sm, k1, ssk, k to end.

Next row (WS): P to end.

Repeat the last 2 rows 4 more times.

When you finish this last row, you should have 64 (72, 72, 76, 78, 82, 82, 82) st on your needles.

Divide these st in 2 halves and place them on 2 different needles. With the RS of the work facing each other, work a 3-needle bind-off over these stitches to close the top of the hood.

Front bands

With US 6 [4 mm] needles, and starting at the bottom of the right front, pick up and knit 94 (94, 94, 94, 104, 104, 104, 104) stitches along the right front, pm, pick up and knit 127 along the hood edge, and 94 (94, 94, 94, 104, 104, 104, 104) stitches along the left front. *315 (315, 315, 315, 335, 335, 335, 335) st.*

Next row (WS): P1, *k1, p1*, repeat to the end of row.

Next row (RS): K1, *p1, k1*, repeat to the end of row.

Sizes 28, 30/32, 34/36, 38/40: **Next row (WS):** P1, *k1, p1* to marker, sm, *yo, p2tog, (k1,p1) 4 times, k1, yo, k2tog, (k1,p1) 4 times, p1*; repeat from * after marker 4 times, yo, p2tog, (k1, p1) twice. *9 buttonholes made.*

Sizes 42/44, 46/48, 50/52, 54/56: **Next row (WS):**

P1, *k1, p1* to marker, sm, yo, k2tog, (p1, k1) 4 times, p1, *yo, p2tog, (k1,p1) 4 times, k1, yo, k2tog, (p1,k1) 4 times, p1*; repeat from * 4 times, yo, p2tog, (k1, p1) twice. *10 buttonholes made.*

Work 2 more rows in k1, p1 ribbing, and on the following row bind off all st in pattern.

Finishing

Weave in ends and block garment to finished measurements. Sew buttons opposite to the button-holes.

Finished Measurements

Bust circumference (incl. subtle gathers): 29¼ (32, 35½, 39¼, 42¾, 47½, 50½, 54¾)" [73 (80, 89, 98, 107, 119, 126, 137) cm].

Bottom circumference at hem: 31 (34, 37½, 41, 44¾, 49½, 52, 56½)" [78 (85, 94, 103, 112, 123, 130, 142) cm].

Armhole depth: 6½ (6¾, 7½, 8½, 8¾, 9½, 10½, 11¼)" [16 (17, 19, 21, 22, 24, 26, 28) cm].

Upper sleeve circumference: 11 (11½, 13, 13¾, 14¾, 16¼, 17½, 18½)" [28 (29, 32, 35, 37, 40½, 44, 46½) cm].

Sleeve length from underarm to cuff: 18½ (19¼, 20, 20, 20, 20½, 20½, 20½)" [46 (48, 50, 50, 50, 51, 51, 51) cm].

Length from underarm to hem: 16 (16½, 17¼, 17¼, 17½, 17½, 17½)" [40 (41, 43, 43, 43, 44, 44, 44) cm].

dipped

by veera välimäki

Designing a cowl is often a search for the perfect stitch pattern and finding just the right one. Dipped is just that cowl. It's simple and effective, holds its shape really well and it's reversible. This cowl will keep you both warm and stylish. Choose your favorite colors and knit away!

Sizes

One size

Finished measurements after blocking: 43" [110 cm] in circumference and 10½" [26 cm] deep.

Materials

Yarn: 3 skeins of Tosh Vintage by Madelinetosh (100% merino wool; 200 yd [182 m] - 100 g); two skeins of MC and one skein of CC. Approx. 600 yd [540 m] of aran weight yarn. Sample is knit in colorways Graphite (gray, MC, two skeins) and Poprocks (pink, CC, one skein).

Needles: US 7 [4.5 mm] circular needle, 24" [60 cm] long. Adjust needle size if necessary to obtain the correct gauge.

Other: Tapestry needle and blocking aids.

Gauge

16 sts and 32 rows = 4" [10 cm] in pattern stitch, unstretched.

Finished Size

43" [110 cm]

10½" [26 cm]

dipped

Cowl

Using circular needle and MC, CO 42 sts. Do not join. *Note: you can use a provisional cast-on if you prefer and use a three-needle bind-off instead of seaming the cast-on edge and bind-off edge together.*

Purl the first row (WS). Work back and forth in pattern stitch as follows. *Note: Stitches increase over few rows and then decrease back to the CO at the end of each 10-row repeat.*

> *Row 1 (RS):* *k3, m1R, k1, m1L, k3; repeat from * to end.

> *Rows 2 and 4 (WS):* purl all stitches.

> *Row 3 (RS):* *k4, m1R, k1, m1L, k4; repeat from * to end.

> *Row 5 (RS):* *k5, m1R, k1, m1L, k5; repeat from * to end.

> *Row 6 (WS):* *ssk, k9, k2tog; repeat from * to end.

> *Rows 7 and 9 (RS):* purl all stitches.

> *Row 8 (WS):* *ssk, k7, k2tog; repeat from * to end.

> *Row 10 (WS):* *ssk, k5, k2tog; repeat from * to end.

Repeat *rows 1-10* until the piece measures 30" [76 cm] ending on a row 10. Change to CC and continue working through *rows 1-10* until the cowl measures 45" [114 cm]. BO all stitches and seam the BO-edge and CO-edge together (or if you used the provisional cast-on, slip the CO stitches on spare needle and join the edges using a three-needle bind-off).

Finishing

Weave in all yarn ends. Block the cowl to measurements, stretching only very lightly.

sheer

Absolute, pure, without a doubt, just simple beauty. like the snow falling from the sky or the sun shining in through your drapes. Seeing clearly what is there even if revealed through a veil of shining fabric. You know what awaits and appreciate its gentle curves and delicate waves. Beckoning you to jump in and enjoy the feminine lacy details and lovely lines.

sheer

fade shawl

thoughts cardigan

thoughts

by joji locatelli

Feminine lines and the lightest, most delicate fabric, meet in this romantic cardigan. Beautiful eyelets slowly move downwards from your shoulders creating a flattering visual effect.

Thoughts is worked seamlessly from the top down, and it can be adapted to any length you prefer.

thoughts

Sizes

XS (S, M, L, XL, XXL, 3XL, 4XL)

Shown in size S. *Note: See more detailed finished measurements below in schematics picture or written on page 77.*

Materials

Yarn: Merino Lace by The Uncommon Thread (100% merino – 656 yd [600 m] – 100 g): 3 (3, 3, 4, 4, 4, 5, 5) skeins. Shown in colorway Pontus.
Needles: US 4 [3.5 mm] and US 2½ [3 mm] circular needles; crochet hook for provisional cast on.
Other: Stitch markers, stitch holders, waste yarn, row counter (optional), 1 hook & eye closure.

Gauge

24 st and 32 rows = 4" [10 cm], on US 4 [3.5 mm] needles, in Stockinette stitch, after blocking.

Finished Measurements

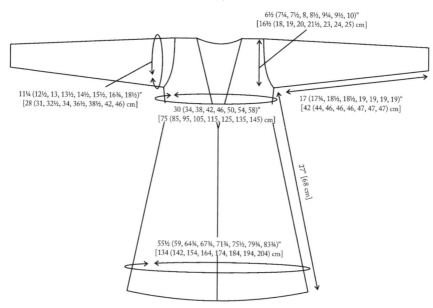

6½ (7¼, 7½, 8, 8½, 9¼, 9½, 10)"
[16½ (18, 19, 20, 21½, 23, 24, 25) cm]

11¼ (12½, 13, 13½, 14½, 15½, 16¾, 18½)"
[28 (31, 32½, 34, 36½, 38½, 42, 46) cm]

30 (34, 38, 42, 46, 50, 54, 58)"
[75 (85, 95, 105, 115, 125, 135, 145) cm]

17 (17¾, 18½, 18½, 19, 19, 19, 19)"
[42 (44, 46, 46, 47, 47, 47) cm]

27" [68 cm]

55½ (59, 64¾, 67¾, 71¾, 75½, 79¾, 83¾)"
[134 (142, 154, 164, 174, 184, 194, 204) cm]

thoughts

Back

With waste yarn and using your US 4 [3.5 mm] needles, provisionally cast on 6 st and work in k1, p1 ribbing until your piece measures 6 (6½, 7, 7½, 7½, 8½, 8½, 8)" [15 (16, 17½, 19, 19, 21, 21, 20) cm]. Break yarn and place these st on hold using a thread of yarn or a safety pin.

Continuing with your US 4 [3.5 mm] needles, provisionally CO 20 (20, 22, 24, 27, 29, 31, 34) stitches. Break waste yarn and leave the provisional stitches on the needle. On the same needle, provisionally CO 20 (20, 22, 24, 27, 29, 31, 34) more stitches. Break waste yarn and leave them on the needle. Now you have two sets of provisional stitches.

Returning to the first set of provisional st, knit them then pick up and knit 36 (40, 42, 46, 46, 50, 50, 48) st along one of the sides of your ribbing band (the side that has a purl column of stitches). Next, knit through the second group of provisional stitches. *You should have 76 (80, 86, 94, 100, 108, 112, 116) sts on the needles.*

Turn work and purl 1 row.

> *Row 1:* K7 (9, 12, 16, 19, 23, 25, 27), [pm, k10] 6 times, pm, k9 (11, 14, 18, 21, 25, 27, 29).

Work 9 rows in Stockinette st.

> *Row 11 – Eyelet Row:* K to m, [sm, k2tog, yo, k8] 6 times, sm, k2tog, yo, k7 (9, 12, 16, 19, 23, 25, 27).

Continue working in pattern repeating the last 10 rows until work measures 5½ (6, 6½, 6¾, 7¼, 8, 8¼, 8½)" [14 (15, 16, 17, 18, 20, 20½, 21) cm] from your provisional CO, ending with a WS row.

Note: Take note of the row number you end on (for example, 3 rows after your last eyelet row). You will now start your armhole shaping. When you work the fronts, start the armhole shaping on the same row, so that your eyelets are placed on the same rows on the back and on the fronts.

Next row (RS): CO2 (2, 3, 3, 3, 4, 4, 4) work in patt to end.

Repeat this row 3 (5, 5, 5, 7, 5, 7, 9) more times (ending with a WS row). *You should now have 84 (92, 104, 112, 124, 132, 144, 156) st.*

Break yarn and put all st (and markers too) on hold.

Right Front

With the RS facing you, unravel the provisional st corresponding to the **Right Shoulder** and place them on the needle. Also place on the needle the stitches you had on hold for that end of your ribbing band (if it was the provisional CO end, unravel them first). *You should have 26 (26, 28, 30, 33, 35, 37, 40) st on the needle.*

Rejoin yarn to begin with a RS row.

> *Row 1 (RS):* K to 6 st before the end of row, (p1, k1) 3 times.
> *Row 2 (WS):* (p1, k1) 3 times, p to end of row.

Work 6 more rows in the established pattern.

> *Row 9 (RS):* Work in patt to 6 st before the end of row, m1L, work in patt to end of row.

As you continue to work the rest of the front, work a neck increase (by m1L) at neck edge on every 4th row from this point on, until you have increased a total of 18 (20, 21, 23, 23, 25, 25, 24) times. *Note: the last neck increases will be made after the armhole shaping and after joining all the pieces together.*

Work 5 more rows in pattern (working neck increases as required).

> *Row 15 (RS):* K5 (6, 8, 10, 13, 15, 17, 20), pm, k2tog, yo, k8, pm, k2tog, yo, work in patt to end of row.

Work 9 rows in pattern, without eyelets (remember to work neck increases as indicated).

> *Row 25 (RS):* [K to m, sm, k2tog, yo] twice, work in patt to end.

Work 9 rows in pattern.

Repeat the last 10 rows once more.

> *Row 45 (RS):* [K to m, sm, k2tog, yo] twice, k8, pm, k2tog, yo, work in patt to end.

Work in this manner, making a Neck Increase every 4th row and an Eyelet Row every 10th row as follows:

> *Eyelet Row:* [K to m, sm, k2tog, yo] 3 times, work in patt to end.

At the same time:

When work measures 6 (6½, 7, 7¼, 7¾, 8½, 8¾,

9)" [15 (16, 17, 18, 19, 21, 21½, 22) cm] from the place where you picked up your stitches, (ending with a WS row -the same you ended up on the back), start Armhole Shaping.

Next row (RS): CO2 (2, 3, 3, 3, 4, 4, 4), work in patt to end.

Next row (WS): Work in patt to end.

Repeat the last 2 rows 1 (2, 2, 2, 3, 2, 3, 4) more times.

Break yarn and put all st (with markers) on hold.

left Front

Unravel the provisional st corresponding to the **Left shoulder** and place them on the needle. Also place on the needle the stitches you had on hold for that end of your ribbing band. *You should have 26 (26, 28, 30, 33, 35, 37, 40) st on the needle.*

Rejoin yarn to begin with a RS row.

Row 1 (RS): (K1, p1) 3 times, k to end of row.

Row 2 (WS): P to 6 st before the end of row, (k1, p1) 3 times.

Work 6 more rows in the established pattern.

Row 9 (RS): (K1, p1) 3 times, m1R, work in patt to end of row.

As you continue to work the rest of the front, work a neck increase (by m1R) at neck edge on every 4th row from this point on, until you have increased a total of 18 (20, 21, 23, 23, 25, 25, 24) times. *Note: the last neck increases will be made after the armhole shaping and after joining all the pieces together.*

Work 5 more rows in pattern (working neck increases as required).

Row 15 (RS): (k1, p1) 3 times, K5 (5, 4, 4, 4, 4, 4, 4), pm, yo, ssk, k8, pm, yo, ssk, k to end.

Work 9 rows in pattern, without eyelets (remember to work neck increases as indicated).

Row 25 (RS): Work in patt to m, sm, yo, ssk, k8, sm, yo, ssk, k to end.

Work 9 rows in pattern.

Repeat the last 10 rows once more.

Row 45 (RS): Work in patt to 10 st before m, pm, [yo, ssk, k8, sm] twice, yo, ssk, k to end.

Work in this manner, making a Neck Increase every 4th row and an Eyelet Row every 10th row as follows:

Eyelet Row: Work in patt to m, sm, [yo, ssk, k8, sm] twice, yo, ssk, k to end.

at the same time:

When work measures 6 (6½, 7, 7¼, 7¾, 8½, 8¾, 9)" [15 (16, 17, 18, 19, 21, 21½, 22) cm] from the place where you picked up your stitches, (ending with a WS row -the same you ended up on the back), start Armhole Shaping.

Next row (RS): Work in patt to end.

Next row (WS): CO2 (2, 3, 3, 3, 4, 4, 4), work in patt to end.

Repeat the last 2 rows 1 (2, 2, 2, 3, 2, 3, 4) more times.

Do not break yarn.

Join all the pieces together

When you join your pieces, transfer all your markers to the needles as well. On this row you will also add side markers. You might want to use special or different colored markers here.

Starting with the foll RS row, work all st from the left front in patt, CO 3 (4, 5, 7, 7, 9, 9, 9), place side marker, CO 3 (4, 5, 7, 7, 9, 9, 9), place the stitches you had on hold from the back onto the needle and work them in pattern, CO 3 (4, 5, 7, 7, 9, 9, 9), place side marker, CO 3 (4, 5, 7, 7, 9, 9, 9), place the stitches you had on hold from the right front on the needle and work them in pattern.

Start working in pattern. By the time you finish your neck increases you should have a total of 192 (212, 240, 264, 288, 312, 336, 360) st. 51 (56, 63, 69, 75, 81, 87, 93) st on each front, and 90 (100, 114, 126, 138, 150, 162, 174) st on the back.

When work measures 4" [10 cm] from the armhole, start Waist Shaping:

Next row (RS) - Waist decrease row: Work in patt to 5 st before side marker, ssk, k3, sm, k3, k2tog, work in patt to 3 st before next side marker, ssk, k3, sm, k3, k2tog. 4 st decreased.

Continue working in patt and repeat a decrease row every 10th row once more. After your last decrease you can remove your side markers, since you are not going to use them anymore.

When work measures 6 "[15 cm] from the armhole, start body increases on the foll Eyelet

Row:

Eyelet/increase row (RS): Work to marker, (sm, yo, ssk, k4, m1L, k to m) twice, sm, yo, ssk, work to next m, (sm, k2tog, yo, k to 4 st before next m, m1R, k4) 3 times, (sm, k2tog, yo, k4, m1L, k to m) 3 times, sm, k2tog, yo, work to next m, (sm, k2tog, yo, k to 4 st before next m, m1R, k4) twice, sm, k2tog, yo, work in patt to end. 10 st increased.

Continue working in pattern, working an *Eyelet/ increase row* every 10th row 14 more times. *You should have 334 (354, 382, 406, 430, 454, 478, 502) st.*

By this time, your work should measure approx. 22½" [57 cm] from your armhole (the garment will stretch more after blocking, when you achieve your blocked gauge). If you want this garment to be longer, you can work some more repeats (always working another set of increases with the *Eyelet rows*). If you want it shorter, you can stop working sooner, you don't need to conclude all increase rows.

On the foll row switch to US 1½ [2.5 mm needles] and work hem:

Next row (RS): (K1, p1) 3 times, k2tog, (p1, k1) to end of row.

Next row (WS): P1, (k1, p1) to end of row.

Work 6 more rows of k1, p1 ribbing, and on the next row bind off all stitches in pattern.

Sleeves

Starting at the center of the lower edge of the sleeve opening and using US 4 [3.5 mm] needles pick up and knit 68 (74, 78, 82, 88, 92, 100, 110) stitches. Place marker. Knit one round.

Row 1: Knit 48 (52, 55, 58, 61, 64, 69, 74), wrap next stitch and turn (W&T – see Glossary).

Row 2: Purl 28 (30, 32, 34, 34, 36, 38, 38), W&T.

Row 3: Knit to wrapped stitch, knit wrap together with wrapped stitch, W&T.

Row 4: Purl to wrapped stitch, purl wrap together with wrapped stitch, W&T.

Repeat *rows 3 and 4* until only 3 (4, 5, 7, 7, 9, 9, 9) stitches remain un-worked at each side of the marker.

Next row: knit to last wrapped stitch, knit wrap together with wrapped stitch, knit to the end of round.

Start knitting in Stockinette stitch in the round.

On the 12th (11th, 10th, 10th, 9th,9th, 9th, 9th) round after the sleeve cap is finished, knit to 2 st before marker, SSK, slip marker, k2tog (2 stitches decreased).

Continue working in Stockinette stitch in the round repeating the decrease round every 12 (11, 10, 8, 7, 7, 6, 5, 4) rounds, a total of 10 (12, 13, 13, 16, 16, 19, 24) times.

48 (50, 52, 56, 56, 60, 62, 62) st remain.

When sleeve measures 14½ (15¼, 16, 16, 16, 16½, 16½, 16½)" [36 (38, 40, 40, 40, 41, 41, 41) cm] (or 2½" [6 cm] before desired length), change to US 2 [2.5 mm] circular needles and work 2½" [6 cm] in k1, p1 ribbing.

Bind off all stitches loosely.

Finishing

Weave in all ends and block the sweater to required measurements, stretching it especially lengthwise so that the fabric will drape more nicely when worn.

Sew the hook & eye closure pieces to the WS of the garment, at the point where your last Neck increase was made.

Finished Measurements

Bust circumference (when worn closed): 30 (34, 38, 42, 46, 50, 54, 58)" [75 (85, 95, 105, 115, 125, 135, 145) cm].

Bottom circumference at hem: 55½ (59, 64¾, 67¾, 71¾, 75½, 79¾, 83¾)" [134 (142, 154, 164, 174, 184, 194, 204) cm].

Armhole depth: 6½ (7¼, 7½, 8, 8½, 9¼, 9½, 10)" [16½ (18, 19, 20, 21½, 23, 24, 25) cm].

Upper sleeve circumference: 11 (11½, 13, 13¾, 14¾, 16¼, 17½, 18½)" [28 (29, 32, 35, 37, 40½, 44, 46½) cm].

Sleeve length from underarm to cuff: 17 (17¾, 18½, 18½, 19, 19, 19, 19)" [42 (44, 46, 46, 46, 47, 47, 47) cm].

Length from underarm to hem: 27" [68 cm].

fade

by veera välimäki

looking for something to keep your shoulders warm in an elegant way? Fade might just be the answer: a light and airy wrap with small delicate details. Its rectangular shape and fading colour play make the simple eyelet-motif travel through the piece.

Sizes

One size

Finished measurements after blocking: 87" [221 cm] wide and 23" [58 cm] deep.

Materials

Yarn: 5 skeins of Supersoft 100% uld by Holst Garn (100% wool; 314 yd [287 m] - 50 g). Approx. 1550 yd [1415 m] of fingering weight yarn, in 4 different colors. Sample is knit in colorways 001 Bleached White (MC, one skein), 043 Alpine Rose (CC1, one skein), 044 Allium (CC2, one skein) and 045 Peony (CC3, two skeins).

Needles: US 4 [3.5 mm] circular needle, 32" [80 cm] long. Adjust needle size if necessary to obtain the correct gauge.

Other: Tapestry needle, stitch markers, and blocking aids.

Gauge

22 sts and 32 rows = 4" [10 cm] in Stockinette stitch.

Finished Size

87" [221 cm]

23"
[58 cm]

fade

Wrap

Using circular needle and MC, CO 120 sts. Do not join. Work in Stockinette stitch until the piece measures 17½" [44 cm] (or until you run out of MC).

Change to CC1 and continue in St st until the piece measures 35" [88 cm] (or until you run out of CC1). *Note: Remember to begin on a RS row at each color change.*

Change to CC2. Work 2" [5 cm] in St st. Continue in St st and place first eyelet motif as follows —

> *Set-up row (RS):* k5, pm, work row 1 of chart A, pm, knit to end.

Work in St st and work through all rows of chart A between first motif markers once. Continue in St st and repeat the *rows 3-18* of the chart A between first motif markers until the piece measures 52½" [132 cm] (or until you run out of CC2).

Change to CC3. Work 1" [2.5 cm] in St st and continue to work through *rows 3-18* of chart A between first motif markers. Continue as established and place second eyelet motifs as follows when you are starting the next *row 17* of the first eyelet motif -

> *Set-up row 2 (RS):* k5, sm, work row 17 of chart A, sm, k until 60 sts remain, pm, work row 1 of chart A twice, pm, knit to end.

Work as established in St st and first and second eyelet motifs and work through all rows of chart A between second motif markers. Continue in St st and eyelet motifs until you have worked *rows 3-18* of the chart between second motif markers 7 times. When you are starting the next *row 17* of the first and second eyelet motif, place third eyelet motifs as follows —

> *Set-up row 3 (RS):* k5, sm, work row 17 of chart A, sm, k to m, sm, work row 17 of chart A twice, sm, k10, pm, work row 1 of chart A twice, pm, knit to end.

Continue in St st and all eyelet motifs until the piece measures 87" [221 cm] (or until you run out of CC3) . BO sts loosely on next row RS).

Finishing

Weave in all yarn ends. Wet block the shawl using wires and pins.

Chart A

		☐	Stockinette stitch; knit on RS, purl on WS
		O	yarn-over
		╱	k2tog
		☐	chart repeat

Note: read the chart from right to left on RS and from left to right on WS.

81

soft

Arguably the nicest feeling of all. like
feathers, a rabbit's soft coat or the smooth
feeling of a baby's skin. Can something feel too
soft? Can a yarn be so sensuous that you
can't stop petting it? We love this sensation
and would gladly spend hours enjoying it,
wrapped up in it.

soft

so close shawl

laneway tunic

so close
by joji locatelli

Quietly soothing fibers and squishy stitches make this beautiful
cozy shawl. Or blanket?
The center square is knit in garter stitch, and the lace border
features a wavy stitch pattern with soft squishy bobbles. Worked
in a delicious alpaca yarn, it makes a luxurious warm accessory
that you will always want to keep close to you.

so close

Sizes

One size.
Finished measurements: 46 x 46" [106 x 106 cm] square.

Materials

Yarn: Baby Alpaca DK by Shibui (100% alpaca; 255 yd [233 m] - 100 g). Main color: 5 skeins (approx. 1150 yd [1050 m]). Contrasting color: 1 skein (aprox. 180 yd [165 m]). Shown in colorways Ash (MC) and Graphite (CC).

Needles: US 7 [4.5 mm] circular or straight needles for the center square and 40" long circular needles for the border. Adjust needle size if necessary to obtain the correct gauge.

Other: Row counter, darning needle for weaving in ends, blocking pins, and wires.

Gauge

15.5 st and 31 rows = 4" [10 cm] in garter stitch, on US 7 [4.5 mm] needles.

Finished Size

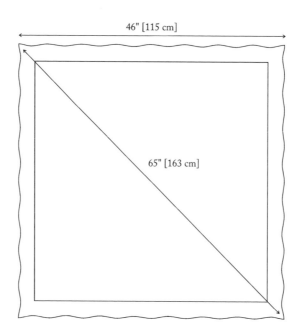

46" [115 cm]

65" [163 cm]

so close

Directions

Center Square

With MC and using US 7 [4.5 mm] circular or straight needles, CO 2 st.

Set-up row: K1, m1, k1.

Next row: Sl1, m1L, k to end.

Repeat this last row until you have 180 st on your needles.

Next row: Sl1, k2tog, k to the end of row.

Repeat this last row until you have only 2 st on the needles. Pass the 1st st over the second one and fasten off.

Striped Band 1

With MC, US 7 [4.5 mm] circular needles and starting on one of the corners, pick up and knit 135 st along the 1st side of your square (you should pick up 3 st for every 4 rows), pm, pick up and knit 135 along each of the other 3 sides, placing a marker on each corner. Make sure you use a different marker for the beginning of the round.

You should have 540 st.

Round 1: Purl all st.

Round 2: *K1, m1L, k to m, m1R, sm* 4 times. You should have 137 on each side between markers (1 corner st + 136 garter st).

Round 3: Purl all st.

Switch to CC. Work rounds 2 and 3 once.

Switch to MC. Work rounds 2 and 3 once.

Repeat the last 4 rounds (including color changes) once more.

You should have 145 st for each side (1 corner st + 144 garter st).

Lace Band

Using MC.

Charted instructions:

Note: see charts on page 91.

Round 1: K1, m1L, work row 1 of Lace Chart

A (repeating the stitches inside the red box 8 times), m1R, sm, k1, m1L, work row 1 of Lace Chart B, m1R, sm, k1, m1L, work row 1 of Lace Chart A, m1R, sm, k1, m1L, work row 1 of Lace Chart B, m1R.

Round 2: Knit all stitches.

Continue working in the established pattern, always working Lace chart A for sides 1 and 3 and Lace chart B for sides 2 and 4. Work in this manner until you have completed all 24 rows of the Lace charts.

Written instructions:

Round 1: [K1, m1L, k3, yo, k1, yo, k1, sssk (see abbreviations), *k3tog, k4, yo, k1, yo, k3, yo, k1, yo, k1, sssk* 8 times, k3tog, k4, yo, k1, yo, m1R, sm, k1, m1L, yo, k1, yo, k4, sssk, *k3tog, k1, yo, k1, yo, k3, yo, k1, yo, k4, sssk* 8 times, k3tog, k1, yo, k1, yo, k3, m1R, sm] twice.

Round 2 and all even-numbered rounds: Knit all stitches.

Round 3: [K1, m1L, k9, *k3tog, k3, yo, k1, yo, k9* 8 times, k3tog, k3, yo, k1, yo, k2, m1R, sm, k1, m1L, k2, yo, k1, yo, k3, sssk, *k9, yo, k1, yo, k3, sssk* 8 times, k9, yo, k1, yo, k3, sssk* 8 times, k9, yo, k1, yo, k3, sssk* 8 times, k9, m1R, sm] twice.

Round 5: [K1, m1L, k6, MB, k3, *k3tog, k2, yo, k1, yo, k6, MB, k3* 8 times, k3tog, k2, yo, k1, yo, k4, m1R, sm, k1, m1L, k4, yo, k1, yo, k2, sssk, *k3, MB, k6, yo, k1, yo, k2, sssk* 8 times, k3, MB, k6, m1R, sm] twice.

Round 7: [K1, m1L, k3, yo, k1, yo, k4, sssk, *k3tog, k1, yo, k1, yo, k3, yo, k1, yo, k4, sssk* 8 times, k3tog, k1, yo, k1, yo, k2, yo, k1, yo, sssk, m1R, sm, k1, m1L, k3tog, yo, k1, yo, k2, yo, k1, yo, k1, sssk, *k3tog, k4, yo, k1, yo, k3, yo, k1, yo, k1, sssk* 8 times, k3tog, k4, yo, k1, yo, k3, m1R, sm] twice.

Round 9: [K1, m1L, k5, yo, k1, yo, k3, sssk, *k9, yo, k1, yo, k3, sssk* 8 times, k8, yo, k1, yo, sssk, m1R, sm, k1, m1L, k3tog, yo, k1, yo, k8, *k3tog, k3, yo, k1, yo, k9* 8 times, k3tog, k3, yo, k1, yo, k5, m1R, sm] twice.

Round 11: [K1, m1L, MB, k6, yo, k1, yo, k2, sssk, *k3, MB, k6, yo, k1, yo, k2, sssk* 8 times, k3, MB, k5, yo, k1, yo, sssk, m1R, sm, k1, m1L, k3tog, yo, k1, yo, k5, MB, k3, *k3tog, k2, yo, k1, yo, k6, MB, k3* 8 times, k3tog, k2, yo, k1, yo, k6, MB, m1R, sm] twice.

Round 13: [K1, m1L, k3tog, k2, yo, k1, yo, k3, yo, k1, yo, k1, sssk, *k3tog, k4, yo, k1, yo, k3, yo, k1, yo, k1, sssk* 8 times, k3tog, k4, yo, k1, yo, k2, yo, k1, yo, sssk, m1R, sm, k1, m1L, k3tog, yo, k1, yo, k2, yo, k1, yo, k4, sssk, *k3tog, k1, yo, k1, yo, k3, yo, k1, yo, k4, sssk* 8 times, k3tog, k1, yo, k1, yo, k3, yo, k1, yo, k2, sssk, m1R, sm] twice.

Round 15: [K1, m1L, k3tog, k2, yo, k1, yo, k9, *k3tog, k3, yo, k1, yo, k9* 8 times, k3tog, k3, yo, k1, yo, k8, m1R, sm, k1, m1L, k8, yo, k1, yo, k3, sssk, *k9, yo, k1, yo, k3, sssk* 8 times, k9, yo, k1, yo, k2, sssk, m1R, sm] twice.

Round 17: [K1, m1L, k3tog, k2, yo, k1, yo, k6, MB, k3, *k3tog, k2, yo, k1, yo, k6, MB, k3* 8 times, k3tog, k2, yo, k1, yo, k6, MB, k3, m1R, sm, k1, m1L, k3, MB, k6, yo, k1, yo, k2, sssk, *k3, MB, k6, yo, k1, yo, k2, sssk* 8 times, k3, MB, k6, yo, k1, yo, k2, sssk, m1R, sm] twice.

Round 19: [K1, m1L, k1, *k3tog, k1, yo, k1, yo, k3, yo, k1, yo, k4, sssk* 10 times, k1, m1R, sm, k1, m1L, k1, *k3tog, k4, yo, k1, yo, k3, yo, k1, yo, k1, sssk* 10 times, k1, m1R, sm] twice.

Round 21: [K1, m1L, k2, *k9, yo, k1, yo, k3, sssk* 10 times, k2, m1R, sm, k1, m1L, k2, *k3tog, k3, yo, k1, yo, k9* 10 times, k2, m1R, sm] twice.

Round 23: [K1, m1L, k3, *k3, MB, k6, yo, k1, yo, k2, sssk* 10 times, k3, m1R, sm, k1, m1L, k3, *k3tog, k2, yo, k1, yo, k6, MB, k3* 10 times, k3, m1R, sm] twice.

Round 24: Knit all st.

By this time you should have 169 st on each side (168 for each lace section + 1 corner st).

Striped Band 2
Using MC.

Round 1: *K1, m1L, k to m, m1R, sm* 4 times. *You should have 171 on each side between markers.*

Round 2: Purl all st.

Switch to CC. Work rounds 1 and 2 once.

Repeat the last 4 rounds (including color changes) once more. *You should have 177 st for each side (1 corner st + 176 garter st).*

Picot bind-off
Using CC, *CO2 using the knitted cast-on, k2tog tbl, k1tbl, pass the first st over the second on right needle, BO2, slip st back to the left needle; repeat from * to the end of row.

Finishing

Weave in ends and block piece to measurements.

Lace chart A (sides 1 and 3)

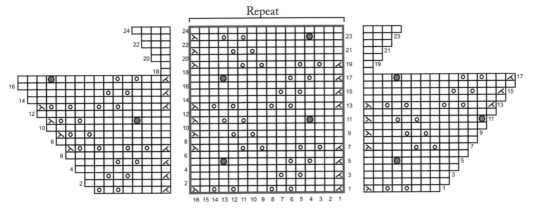

Lace chart B (sides 2 and 4)

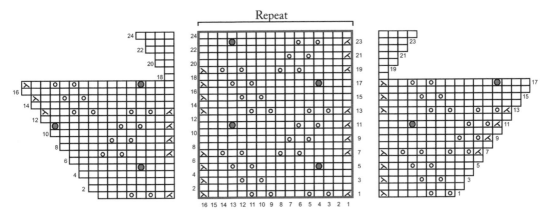

Legend to the charts:

☐ Knit

☐ Yarn over

◩ Slip 3 stitches, one by one, to the RN, insert LN through the front loop of all 3 and knit them together.

◨ K3tog

● Bobble: (K1, k1tbl, k1, k1tbl, k1), all into the same st. Turn work. Sl1, p 4. Turn work. Sl1, k4. Turn work. P2tog, p1, p2tog. Turn work. Sl 2 as if to k2tog, k1, pass slipped st over.

laneway

by veera välimäki

laneway is a strikingly graphic tunic. It feels like a light
breath on your skin, but keeps you wonderfully warm
and cozy. Softness at its best! And if you look closely,
you can find a little splash of color in this otherwise
monochromatic design.

laneway

Sizes

XS (S, M, L, XL, XXL)

Finished chest circumference: 30 (34, 38, 42, 46, 50)" [75 (85, 95, 105, 115, 125) cm]. Choose a size with no ease.

Materials

Yarn: 4 (4, 5, 5, 6, 6) skeins of Lush Twist by The Uncommon Thread (80% superwash merino, 10% cashmere, 10% nylon; 400 yd [365 m] - 100 g), 3 (3, 4, 4, 5, 5) skeins in MC and 1 skein in CC1 and a partial skein of CC2. Approx. 1220 (1340, 1480, 1620, 1740, 1860) yards [1120 (1210, 1350, 1480, 1590, 1700) m] of fingering weight yarn. Sample is knit in colorways Breath (gray, MC), Coven (black, CC1) and Pow! (pink, CC2), in size small.

Needles: US 2½ [3 mm] and US 4 [3.5 mm] circular needle - 32" [80 cm] long, and dpns. Adjust needle size if necessary to obtain the correct gauge.

Other: Tapestry needle, stitch markers in two colors, stitch holders / waste yarn, and blocking aids.

Gauge

24 sts and 32 rows = 4" [10 cm] in Stockinette stitch using larger needle.

Finished Size

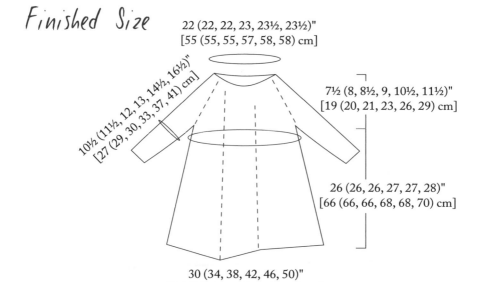

22 (22, 22, 23, 23½, 23½)"
[55 (55, 55, 57, 58, 58) cm]

10½ (11½, 12, 13, 14½, 16½)"
[27 (29, 30, 33, 37, 41) cm]

7½ (8, 8½, 9, 10½, 11½)"
[19 (20, 21, 23, 26, 29) cm]

26 (26, 26, 27, 27, 28)"
[66 (66, 66, 68, 68, 70) cm]

30 (34, 38, 42, 46, 50)"
[75 (85, 95, 105, 115, 125) cm]

laneway

Collar

Using smaller circular needle and MC, CO 132 (132, 132, 136, 140, 140) sts. Place marker for beginning of round and join carefully, not twisting your sts. Work 1" [2.5 cm] in twisted ribbing (*k1 through back loop, p1; repeat from * to end of round).

Yoke

Change to larger circular needle and continue in Stockinette stitch. Begin raglan increases and shape the neck with short rows.

Set-up round (RS): sm, k 20 (16, 12, 10, 10, 10), pm, k 46 (50, 54, 58, 60, 60), pm, k 20 (16, 12, 10, 10, 10), pm, k 46 (50, 54, 58, 60, 60) to end.

Short row 1 (RS): *sm, k1, m1L, k until 1 st before next marker remains, m1R, k1; repeat twice from *, sm, k1, m1L, k2, turn work.

Short row 2 (WS): yo, *purl to m, sm; repeat three times from *, p1, m1RP, p2, turn work.

Short row 3 (RS): yo, k to m, *sm, k1, m1L, k until 1 st before next marker remains, m1R, k1; repeat twice from *, sm, k1, m1L, k to previous yarn-over, k2tog the yarn-over with the next stitch, k1, turn work.

Short row 4 (WS): yo, *purl to m, sm; repeat three times from *, p1, m1RP, p to previous yarn-over, ssp the yarn-over with the next stitch, p1, turn work.

Repeat the **short rows 3 and 4** three more times. Work to end of round (RS): yo, k to m.

Begin raglan increases, stripes and the slant at the front (decrease/increase). *Note: Add different colored markers for the front slant in the following set-up round. Pick up the last two remaining yarn-overs on set-up round (k2tog the first yarn-over with the next stitch and ssk the second yarn-over with the*

previous stitch).

Set-up round (RS, MC): *sm, k1, m1L, k until 1 st before next marker remains, m1R, k1; repeat twice from *, sm, k1, m1L, k2, pm, k until 10 sts remain before end of the round remains, pm, k until 1 st before next marker remains, m1R, k1 to end.

Round 1 (RS, MC): *sm, k to m; repeat from * five times, k to end.

Round 2 (RS, MC; increase round): *sm, k1, m1L, k until 1 st before next marker remains, m1R, k1; repeat twice from *, sm, k1, m1L, k to m, sm, m1L, k until two stitches before next m remain, k2tog, sm, k until 1 st before next marker remains, m1R, k1 to end.

Round 3 (RS, CC): *sm, k to m; repeat from * five times, k to end.

Round 4 (RS, MC; increase round): *sm, k1, m1L, k until 1 st before next marker remains, m1R, k1; repeat twice from *, sm, k1, m1L, k to m, sm, m1L, k until two stitches before next m remain, k2tog, sm, k until 1 st before next marker remains, m1R, k1 to end.

Repeat the **rounds 1 to 4** — 7 (9, 11, 13, 15, 18) more times and work **rounds 1 and 2** — 0 (0, 0, 0, 1, 1) more time [*308 (340, 372, 408, 452, 500) stitches on needle*].

Divide for body and sleeves

Note: work with the right color to keep the striping continuous for your size.

(RS): Slip marker, place all stitches before next marker to holder/waste yarn, remove marker, k to marker, slip marker, place all stitches before next marker to holder/waste yarn, remove marker, k to marker, sm, knit to marker, sm, knit to end.

You have 180 (204, 228, 252, 276, 300) stitches on needle for body and 64 (68, 72, 78, 88, 100) stitches on each holder for sleeves.

Body

Work in the round in Stockinette stitch and continue striping (1 round in CC, 3 rounds in MC) and front slant (increases/decreases) every second round as established. When body measures 2" [5 cm] from underarm, begin increases on a slant round.

Increase round: sm, k4, m1L, k until 4 sts

before next marker remain, m1R, k4, sm, k4, m1L, k to m, sm, m1L, k until 2 sts before next m remain, k2tog, sm, k until 4 sts before next marker remain, m1R, k4.

Work the *increase round* on every 4th round and continue striping and front increases/decreases as established until the body measures 13" [33 cm] from underarm ending with a non-slant round.

Continue in MC only, working St st and add pockets. Work the back piece only: k to m and turn. Work 5" [12 cm] back and forth in Stockinette stitch (k on RS, p on WS), working only the back stitches between side markers and ending with a RS row. Cut yarn and re-attach to the front stitches. Work 5" [12 cm] back and forth in Stockinette stitch and front slant as established every other row, working only the front stitches between side markers and ending with a RS row.

> *Join in round again (RS):* sm, k the back stitches, sm, knit the front stitches.

Continue in St st and work the front slant every other round as established, until the body measures 24½ (24½, 24½, 25½, 25½, 26½)" [63 (63, 63, 65, 65, 67) cm] from underarm.

Change to smaller needle and work 1½" [3 cm] in twisted ribbing.

Sleeves

Note: work with the right color to keep the striping continuous for your size. You can also pick up a few additional stitches from underarm to prevent a hole, or sew the hole while finishing. Decrease these additional stitches on next possible round.

Place 64 (68, 72, 78, 88, 100) sleeve sts from holder on larger dpns. Re-attach right yarn for continuous striping, place a marker to mark the beginning of the round and join. Work in Stockinette stitch and continue striping (1 round in CC, 3 rounds in MC) until sleeve measures 4" [10 cm] from underarm.

> *Decrease round:* k2, ssk, k until 4 sts remain, k2tog, k to end.

Repeat the *decrease round* twice every 2" [5 cm]. Work striping in Stockinette stitch until sleeve measures 17" [30 cm] from underarm. Change to smaller dpns and with MC yarn, continue in twisted ribbing for additional 1" [2.5 cm] . BO sleeve sts loosely in twisted ribbing.

Pockets

Using smaller dpns and CC2, with RS of the tunic facing and start from the bottom of the pocket slit and pick up and knit 28 sts up to top of the pocket slip, pm, pick up and knit 28 sts down the other edge of the pocket slit [*56 sts on needle*].

Join in round placing a marker for beginning of round and work in Stockinette stitch and slant the pocket piece as follows —

> *Round 1 (increase/decrease round):* k1, m1L, knit until 3 sts before next marker remain, k2tog, k1, sm, k1, ssk, knit until 1 stitch before end of round remain, m1R, k1.
>
> *Round 2 and 4:* knit all stitches.
>
> *Round 3 (increase round):* k1, m1L, knit to marker, sm, knit until 1 stitch before end of round remain, m1R, k1.

Repeat *rounds 1 to 4* until the pocket measures 6" [15 cm]. Turn the pocket to inside (WS of the pocket facing), divide st evenly on two dpns and BO using 3-needle bind-off technique.

Finishing

Weave in all yarn ends. Block the tunic using your preferred method. If necessary, you can sew one corner of the pockets on WS to make them stay in place.

glossary

glossary of terms and useful links

Wrap and Turn
A great tutorial by The Purl Bee on short rows can be found here:
http://www.purlbee.com/2008/06/18/short-rows/

Provisional Cast On
I use the crochet provisional cast on. There is a great tutorial by Lucy Neatby on YouTube. I find it extremely clear and I love to use this technique because I end up will all my provisional stitches on the needle:
http://www.youtube.com/watch?v=R3J-sUx_whE

Elastic Bind-Off
Knit 1, *knit next st, insert left needle through the front loops of both st on your right needle and knit them together through the back loop*, repeat to the end of row.

abbreviations

approx:	Approximately
BO:	Bind Off
CC:	Contrasting Color
C2B:	Place 1 st on CN, hold at WS of the work, knit next 1 st, knit 1 from CN.
C2F:	Place 1 st on CN, hold at RS of the work, knit next 1 st, knit 1 from CN.
C4B:	Place 2 sts on CN, hold at WS of the work, knit next 2 sts, knit 2 from CN.
C4F:	Place 2 sts on CN, hold at RS of the work, knit next 2 sts, knit 2 from CN.
C6B:	Place 3 sts on CN, hold at WS of the work, knit next 3 sts, knit 3 from CN.
C6F:	Place 3 sts on CN, hold at RS of the work, knit next 3 sts, knit 3 from CN.
CO:	Cast On
foll(s):	Follows, following
Garter st:	Garter stitch; Back and forth: knit on RS and WS; In the round: knit one round; purl one round
k:	Knit
k1fb:	Knit into front of the stitch, leave stitch on left needle and knit into back of the same stitch; increase
k2tog:	Knit 2 sts together; decrease
kfbf:	knit through the front, back, and then front again
LN:	Left needle.
m:	Marker
MC:	Main Color
MB:	Make Bobble: Kfbf (knit through the front, back, and then front again) into the same st, turn work. P3, turn work. K3. Slip 2nd and 3rd st on the RN, one by one, over the 1st one.
m1p:	Purled increase. With left needle tip, lift strand between needles, from back to front. Purl lifted loop.
m1Rp:	Right slanting increase, make one right; pick up the strand between the stitches from back, purl through th front of the stitch.
m1Lp:	Left slanting increase, make one left; pick up the strand between the stitches from front, purl through the back of the stitch.
m1L:	Increase slanted to the left (pick up the horizontal bar btw the sts from front to back, knit through back leg)
m1R:	Increase slanted to the right (pick up the horizontal bar btw the sts from back to front, knit through front leg)
patt:	Pattern
pm:	Place marker
p:	Purl
p1fb:	Purl into front of the stitch, leave stitch on left needle and purl into back of the same stitch; increase.
p2tog:	Purl 2 sts together; decrease
pwise:	Purlwise
RS:	Right side
rev St st:	Reverse Stockinette stitch; knit on WS, purl on RS.
sl:	Slip
sm:	Slip marker
ssk:	Slip, slip, knit slipped sts tbl; decrease
ssp:	Slip, slip, purl slipped sts tbl; decrease
st(s):	Stitch (stitches)
St st:	Stockinette stitch; knit on RS, purl on WS.
tbl:	Through back loop
tog:	Together
WS:	Wrong side
W&T:	Wrap and turn; work to place stated in pattern, bring yarn front, slip the next st without knitting it, bring the yarn back, slide the slipped st back on left needle, and turn work.
yo:	Yarn over